This book is due for return on or before the last date shown above but it may be renewed by personal application, post, or telephone, quoting this date and the book number.

HERTFORDSHIRE COUNTY LIBRARY
COUNTY HALL, HERTFORD.

L.32

MRS. GASKELL

MRS. GASKELL

by

YVONNE FFRENCH

" C'est le romancier des cas de conscience."
É. MONTÉGUT.

London

HOME & VAN THAL LTD.

Cb1173878

First published 1949

PRINTED IN GREAT BRITAIN BY
MORRISON AND GIBB LTD., LONDON AND EDINBURGH
FOR HOME AND VAN THAL LTD., 36 GREAT RUSSELL STREET LONDON, W.C.I

ACKNOWLEDGMENT

My thanks are due to Messrs. Longmans, Green & Co. Limited for kindly allowing me to quote a passage from *Memorials of Two Sisters*, by M. Shaen.

Y. ff.

ELIZABETH CLEGHORN GASKELL was born at Chelsea in 1810. On the narrow-fronted house [1] overlooking the Thames at Battersea Bridge, a tablet records her birth. It records nothing more : a year later when her mother had died, the infant, confided to the care of her aunt, had been taken by stage-coach to Knutsford. Here in her natural setting she developed. London was to possess her no longer. It was to be nothing but a birthplace and, later, the scene of an unhappy memory. Long afterwards, infrequently, it was to welcome her cordial presence as a celebrity.

This forcible removal was no transplantation. Now it even appears as an inevitable fragment of the Grand Design. Henceforward the child and the scene are complementary, uniting harmoniously in congenial soil : the one creating, the other perpetuating. Her influences, carefully balanced, are seen to be both environal and hereditary.

Her father, William Stevenson, of seafaring stock and Scandinavian extraction had married a Holland ; of a family established at Sandlebridge in Cheshire for generations. Both parties sprang from the middle class ; sturdiness and independence were their framework. Their background was sober, woven with the robust fabric of Dissent. They were Unitarians ; William Stevenson as a youth had been intended for the Ministry. His career had some influence on the literary work of his daughter ; it was restless and unsatisfactory, but varied.

[1] 93 Cheyne Walk ; then, 12 Lindsey Row.

A slight literary thread already twisted through the family skein. A remote connection with the author of *The Seasons* could be established. This may or may not have influenced Stevenson's tastes. At all events he was markedly studious at school, scholarly at his Theological college, and by the time he was twenty had been classical tutor at Manchester Academy, and afterwards Minister at Failsworth Chapel. Here in 1792, and in the hey-day of Nonconformism two influences altered his ideas and settled his future. They proceeded from two friends, and were embodied in the Reverend George Wicke, and Dr. Thomas Barnes, D.D. Mr. Wicke developed certain qualms of conscience which decided him to refuse remuneration for preaching, to declare his principles in a pamphlet, and to support them by resigning his ministry.

It was the age of principle. Convictions above all counted with thoughtful men. And the sacrifice of a career was the price of an easy conscience.

The precedent was enough to disquiet that of William Stevenson. Troubled by similar scruples, as they will be found later disturbing the conscience of Mr. Hale [1] he, too, on similar grounds left the Ministry.

The influence of Dr. Barnes led also to developments. Though in themselves less drastic their results were positive. Intimate with the Hollands, Dr. Barnes was the medium through which Stevenson met Elizabeth Holland who, in 1797, became his wife. Thereafter, completely secularised, Stevenson went to live in East Lothian where, adopting scientific farming, he experimented with a friend, James Cleghorn.

This was an unlucky venture. Agricultural experiments

[1] *North and South.*

were foredoomed at the height of a continental war. All the familiar setbacks embarrassed the enthusiast. Invasion scares, financial panics, bad harvests and the rest. It ended, as it was bound to end, in failure. Agriculture was dropped in favour of boarding and coaching university students in Edinburgh. This, too, was an enterprise of short duration. Before long Stevenson had turned to journalism, and edited the *Scots Magazine*, contributing also to the *Edinburgh Review*. Yet after three years he was again prepared for a change of occupation. It came about in a manner not entirely of his own seeking. His friend Lord Lauderdale was instrumental in procuring a post for him ; that of Keeper of the Treasury Records. This brought him and his family up to London.

There had been a moment when it looked as if Lauderdale might have been going to India as Governor-General ; taking Stevenson with him as his private secretary. The moment, however, passed and instead of India he had to be content with Chelsea. This post appears to have suited him ; he retained it for life. And in due course his wife lay in at their house in Cheyne Walk. Here, on September 29, 1810, was born her last child, a daughter. She was named Elizabeth after her mother, and after her father's old associate in East Lothian, Cleghorn. Not long afterwards the Stevensons moved to Beaufort Street. Here the mother died, just over a year later. She appears to have been delicate. Possibly eight childbirths and a restless existence had done little to strengthen her constitution. William Stevenson, a year-old baby on his hands, looked round helplessly for assistance and turned, perhaps inevitably, to his sister-in-law, Hannah Lumb.

Mrs. Lumb, *née* Holland, was a resident of Knutsford. Prosperous, kindly and comfortable, she lived in a large house on the heath with her crippled daughter, for Mr. Lumb had gone out of his mind and was elsewhere.

It was thus that William Stevenson's child was sent to live with her aunt who became, as things turned out, a second mother. Her heathside house became Elizabeth's home, the cripple her sister. Near by was Sandlebridge, the Holland stronghold, a nest of cousins. Sandlebridge, as well as Knutsford, is the inspiring background for the rural idylls in those of the novels and tales which are pastoral in character.

Elizabeth Stevenson's youth at Knutsford was happy and sheltered. She lived the restrained life of her relatives ; accompanied Dr. Peter Holland, her uncle, on his diurnal rounds, invested him with enduring qualities and later created in his memory the pattern of the old-fashioned country doctor. She was trained in the way she should go by a number of old aunts and uncles : devout Unitarians all, and zealous in the practice of their principles. She worshipped in Chapel, taught in Sunday School, played with her cousins, gazed into the mill-race, dreamed among the corn-shocks, devoured old tales and gradually grew.

Only one discordant note in this protected existence seems to have disturbed her youth. This was struck by intermittent visits to London to stay at her father's, where, since his remarriage in 1814 to a Catherine Thomson, there were now two more children in a household which lacked harmony.

When she was nearly fifteen she was sent to Avonbank School, kept by the Misses Byerley, one of whom was connected by marriage with her stepmother. The Avonbank curriculum appears to have been of a high order ; she remained there for two years without going home, and was taught languages, deportment and etiquette. Its standards were exalted, if the deportment of the young ladies in *My Lady Ludlow* is representative. At any rate she was there until 1827, when she returned to Knutsford. Soon after this she was called to London by the news that her brother, John Stevenson, had unaccountably vanished while on a sea voyage. He was never heard of again. The news broke her father. In failing health and disheartened spirits he wished for his daughter's company. She joined the Beaufort Street household, and for two years one of those distressing periods followed which became so deeply impressed on her memory. At the end of that time her father died.

There was evidently no question that she should remain on with her stepmother. Elizabeth moved to Park Lane for a time with her uncle, Swinton Holland, but visiting Sir Henry Holland in Lower Brook Street.

That same autumn, 1829, she went back for a short time to Mrs. Lumb, but whatever the reason she was not to be at Knutsford for long. Other plans had been arranged through the assiduity of her relations. A cousin of the first Mrs. Stevenson had married a Unitarian Minister, distinguished for many reasons, the Rev. William Turner. A widower, Mr. Turner lived at Newcastle-on-Tyne with his daughter Ann, and there is reason to think that Elizabeth went to this household primarily as a companion to this young cousin.

The character of Mr. Turner's household, of his profound charity and faith, as well as the circumstance of the cholera epidemic which struck Newcastle a year or so later, were all shrewdly observed and later embodied in *Ruth*. In Thurstan Benson, a Christ-like humanitarian who puts principles above wordly advantage, a height of idealism is reached which is unsurpassed in her other novels.

At the outbreak of cholera Elizabeth and Ann were packed off to Edinburgh for some months, but eventually came down to Manchester on a visit to a Mrs. Robberds, William Turner's elder daughter. Her husband was Minister of Cross Street Unitarian Chapel, and had a promising assistant, William Gaskell, a grave young man who was to distinguish himself in many ways in that time of Nonconformist zeal and intellectual brilliance. Scholarly and eloquent, eventually the magnet of his congregation, he became Professor of English History and Literature at Manchester New College, was an able German scholar, an authority on the Lancastrian dialect, a hymn-writer and latterly Editor of the *Unitarian Herald*.

Still, in 1832, he was only twenty-seven. In appearance he was tall and distinguished, and in character very grave and serious. That he fell in love with Elizabeth Stevenson was, on the whole, not surprising. She was engaging, she was a beauty ; she was extremely entertaining and immensely active. A certain surprise is perceptible, however, through the good-natured raillery of Mrs. Lumb : " How could the man ever take a fancy to such a little giddy, thoughtless thing as you ? " she wrote to her niece. But her approval was evidently unconditional. The preparations were put in hand ; the marriage took place on August 30 of the same year, at Knutsford ; and after a wedding-breakfast at Mrs. Lumb's, Mr. and Mrs. Gaskell set off upon their married life.

First of all they went to Festiniog, in Wales.

II

THE wedding journey was over. Exactly a month
later it was time to return to Manchester, to earnest
life and sober duty. Mr. Gaskell had previously
secured a house in Dover Street, modest and unpretentious,
befitting their means, convenient also to his work. His
wife, too, embarked upon responsibilities of her own. At
Knutsford, already, she had gained some experience in social
work. Lessons in Sunday School, charitable errands,
cottage visits and the like had been regarded as natural
activities in young women of respectable upbringing and
recognised circumstances. But the lot of the minister's wife
in the 'thirties, in Manchester as in most of the industrial
north, was an education in realities. It meant coming to
grips with problems that could not be solved, misery that
could not be alleviated, injustices that cried aloud for
equitable settlements. All this stirred Mrs. Gaskell to a
passion of sympathy ; times indeed were enough to challenge
humanitarian instincts to their utmost, but hers, although
strong, were not yet ripe for expression.

During her early married life she had little occasion for
any activity unconnected with domestic or parochial duties.
Life was a dedication to husband and parishioners, home
and children. For babies soon now began to make their
appearance in Dover Street. First, in 1833, and to her great
grief, a stillborn daughter, the subject of her earliest recorded
lines : " On Visiting the Grave of My Stillborn Little
Girl." In the following year was born her eldest child,
Marianne.

In 1837 another daughter was born, Margaret Emily, known as Meta, and the same year saw the death of kind Mrs. Lumb, and marked the convenient inheritance of an annuity of £80 from her estate and a reversionary interest in the residue after the death of another aunt, Abigail Holland.

It was, on the whole, a busy, fervent, unsophisticated period. Occasional visits to Knutsford broke the routine with their calm and there were holidays enjoyed in remote villages farther north, or by the sea. Yet these were only short variations from the discouraging parochial scene : Manchester was always overpoweringly in the background, calling through smoke and grime to Mr. Gaskell ; beckoning him back to his books and his study, his sermons and translations. Manchester throbbing unceasingly through soot and rain, was strong, resilient, pulsating with energy and ruthless in exaction. Mrs. Gaskell, with her gay heart and enterprising ways looking about for some outlet to her imaginative ideas, began to understand something of the remorseless nature of the thousand looms that demanded groans for bread, and tears for water. Ideas, long felt, began to germinate.

There were other aspects than these to Manchester life. A prosperous, intellectual and progressive society had formed there, actively philanthropic and of a high cultural standard.

Influential families, German as well as English, made a point of supporting Nonconformist congregations. And of these the cream was to be found among the Unitarians. Particularly so in Mr. Gaskell's congregation. An objective comment comes from Susanna

Winkworth, bred in the Church of England and versed in theology :

> The Unitarians in Manchester were as a body far away superior to any other in intellect, culture and refinement of manners. . . .[1]

The Winkworths had settled in Manchester shortly before Mrs. Gaskell's marriage : a cultured family, brimming with intellectual precocity. From Mr. Gaskell the daughters received lessons in literature, Greek and Science ; from James Martineau in mental philosophy. Two of them survived : Catherine, a rare and accomplished spirit, as the author of *Lyra Germanica* ; Susanna as the translator of Bunsen and Niebuhr. For Mrs. Gaskell portrayed at this period we are indebted to their memoirs [1] :

> When we first knew Mrs. Gaskell she had not yet become celebrated, but from the earliest days of our intercourse with her we were struck with her genius, and used to say to each other that we were sure she could write books, or do anything else in the world that she liked. And the more we knew of her the more we admired her. . . .
>
> . . . All her great intellectual gifts—her quick, keen observation, her marvellous memory, her wealth of imaginative power, her rare felicity of instinct, her graceful and racy humour—were so warmed and brightened by sympathy and feeling, that while actually with her you were less conscious of her power than of her charm. No one ever came near her in the gift of telling a story. . . . When, a few years later, all the world was admiring her novels, we felt that what she had actually published was a mere fraction of what she might have written, had her life been a less many-sided one ; so that fine as it was it scarcely gave an adequate idea of her highest powers ; but her other occupation left her little time for literary work. Her books, indeed, were only written when all possible domestic and social claims had been satisfied.

[1] *Memorials of Two Sisters.* Shaen. Longmans, Green, 1908.

The first excursion into print had been tentative and anonymous. In 1836 Mrs. Gaskell, far from strong, and expecting the birth of her daughter, Meta, had tried her hand at a little writing.

In the January number of *Blackwood's* for 1837 a set of verses appeared entitled *Sketches Among the Poor* (No. 1), a collaboration of both husband and wife. Mr. Gaskell, with his leanings to versification and known regard for Crabbe, may be considered responsible for the manner and technique ; his wife for the subject and the characteristic approach. Some years later in her correspondence she admitted the authorship : " We once," she wrote, " thought of trying to write *Sketches Among the Poor* rather in the manner of Crabbe . . . but in a more seeing-beauty spirit, and one, the only one—was published in *Blackwood*. But I suppose we spoke our plan near a dog-rose for it never went any further."

Superstitions apart, and Mrs. Gaskell's references to local superstitions are frequent throughout all her work, these verses, beginning and ending as they did with the first number, were intended as a series of poems dealing with Manchester types, based upon Crabbe's methods in *Tales of the Hall*.

The sole interest to-day of this preliminary swallow is that it traces the lines, later more fully developed, of old Alice in *Mary Barton*. The pathos surrounding this touching character is less effective in verse than in its final form which naturally gave greater scope for display of sentiment. The theme, a loyalty to friends, all of whom are united in their deep distress, prevents the old woman from the selfish wish to revisit the countryside of her youth. Her sense of duty is developed with intense emotion. Liberation, when finally achieved, comes only with the release through sleep—or death—of the enchained soul. Dreams are the reward ; blessings in which

> She wandered far and wide
> Among the hills, her sister at her side—
> That sister slept beneath a grassy tomb.

There is nothing to commend these lines : they are poor, mawkish and conventional. But they are interesting because they prove beyond doubt that more than ten years before the publication of her first novel ideas for its minor characters were, at any rate, forming in her mind. Had *Sketches Among the Poor* been continued they might and probably would have included further studies of characters which later appeared in the novel.

Attempts have been made to ascribe the influences which produced *Mary Barton* to some of its immediate precursors. As late as the 'thirties very little had been done by writers to force public attention to social evils, or to realise the living conditions of the poor. But after that the trickle began. Mrs. Trollope's *Michael Armstrong, The Factory Boy* in 1840, was followed in 1844 by *Coningsby*, and in 1845 by *Sybil*. Disraeli's " Blue Book in Fiction," as it is called by Mr. G. M. Young, although achieving an object of sorts by focusing public attention on the immense division existing between rich and poor, can hardly be claimed as humanitarian for its own sake. It used a social means to serve a political end : it presented a theme and proposed a remedy.

There were other efforts : not all successful. Douglas Jerrold's play, *The Factory Girl*, was a failure. Harriet Martineau's *Illustrations of Political Economy* embraced the subject but lacked the imaginative appeal of fiction. And there is no evidence that Mrs. Gaskell had read any of these

early examples, or that she had been influenced by their
dawning efforts at reform. What is certain is that *Sketches
Among the Poor* was an independent though still, small
voice, and that in *Mary Barton* Mrs. Gaskell followed a line
of her own based on conclusions reached from personal
experience and observation. Hers is the first voice to plead
the cause of humanity solely for humanitarian ends.

While she had been at school she had seen something
of the neighbourhood of Stratford-on-Avon. A taste for
topography, inborn, was derived from her father, and joined
to his leanings toward antiquarianism. An old moated
house, a ruin, a mouldering tower, produced reactions which
while not exactly poetical had strong emotional and literary
affinities. From Avonbank she had with the other girls
been taken to visit Clopton House, a decaying mansion, still
partly inhabited, but with history echoing through its rafters
and relics in almost every room. The impressions it made
had been intense and dramatic : she was attracted to ruins.
When, therefore, in 1838 she read of a book in preparation by
William Howitt, famous for his literary peregrinations, Mrs.
Gaskell was put in mind of this visit to Clopton House. She
wrote to Howitt asking whether he, too, knew the place,
and her recollection drew forth a flow of descriptive writing
that impressed him by its warmth and fluency.

Two years later, in *Visits to Remarkable Places*, he included
her account of Clopton House in full, with acknowledg-
ments to " a fair lady." This encouragement was followed
up by a long letter enjoining her to devote herself to writing.

Whatever remained of the " little giddy, thoughtless "
exterior, seriousness ran deep through her nature. If at this
date she set aside Howitt's advice as impracticable it was
because, in the life of a Victorian minister's lady, there was,

so far, little place for self-expression, less for self-indulgence
and no room for her own.

Time passed, and their circumstances advanced. The need
for strict economy was no longer quite so urgent, nor the
privations so acute. Mr. Gaskell's stipend had been increased,
and the annuity from Mrs. Lumb improved domestic conditions. In 1841 a continental holiday was determined on,
and the Gaskells went abroad. They journeyed up the
Rhine. It was here that they fell in with the Howitts, and
began a lasting friendship. With impressions of the Clopton
letter still in his memory Howitt renewed his advice to Mrs.
Gaskell on the desirability of a literary career. Yet still his
words were not realised. Literary wives were luxuries no
early Victorian minister of religion could afford. For one
thing there was nowhere they might write, for another
there was no knowing what they might choose to write
about. The project was put aside, with a cheerful sigh. No
more for the time being was thought about it.

In 1842 another daughter was born, Florence Elizabeth.
The house in Dover Street, now ten years inhabited, was
becoming crowded. With expanding circumstances they
moved to 121 Upper Rumford Street.

So far the Gaskells had three daughters. A son, constantly
hoped for, was born in October 1844. The next year, his
mother took him with Marianne for the summer holiday to
Wales. Festiniog with its sentimental associations was again
chosen, unluckily as it turned out, for here Marianne caught
scarlet fever. It was a slight attack : she recovered. But
death placed a frigid hand on little William who next
succumbed at Portmadoc to which they had moved for
Marianne's convalescence. By August 10, he was dead.

For Mrs. Gaskell the crisis that followed was of a character to influence her whole future. Devotion like hers, concentrated in strength upon a particular child, has a tragic intensity. At times she was hardly expected to survive the shock. For weeks, seriously ill, she was in a state of prostration. Her health, never robust, was almost shattered. Fatigue, anxiety and illness had ended in the void of death. For a time the numbing effects seemed almost to have undermined her constitution, and as week followed week of lassitude without apparent improvement in her condition, efforts were made by her husband to rouse her. It was felt that, failing distraction, succumb she must. And then, remembering her interests, Mr. Gaskell had an idea. He suggested, he persuaded her to begin writing once again.

The remedy worked.

In development she was late. Subconsciously feeling her way by degrees she instinctively groped for the opportunity to express her nature fully. When it arrived the form it took was unexpected, its circumstances strangely sad.

Brooding over the loss of the little boy it is likely that grief expressed itself in a latent compassion for the infinitely vaster tragedy unrolling around her. Undoubtedly she needed distraction ; but in her new-found maturity the realities with which she was confronted in that dark Manchester of the 'forties, added to personal sorrow, drove her into articulate expression through her first cry of human indignation : *Mary Barton.*

III

M ARY BARTON is a story of Manchester, and the history of early nineteenth-century Manchester is the history of aggressive industrialism outstripping social and philanthropic reform.

In the North of England, distress, chronic since the introduction of the Corn Laws, had been aggravated by the resultant flow of populations from the depressed countryside into congested urban areas. It festered on through the 'twenties, but during the 'thirties gradually grew worse. By 1836 over-production at home and an economic depression in America reaped a ghastly harvest of mass unemployment, poverty, hunger and despair. Half Lancashire closed down ; overnight thousands were destitute. Overcrowding in areas already insanitary led to epidemics ; whole districts became pestilential. Swarming towns, ill-adapted for rapid social changes, were unprepared for the accommodation of vast, resentful and despairing throngs. The closing of mills through lack of markets was, to the workers, incomprehensible. Official aid, frequently invoked, had remained unsympathetic.

Finally, in 1839, the rejection of the Chartists' petition had led to sullen resentment ; talk was all of force, violence and revolution. But in the end, and perhaps never seriously apprehended, the movement petered out, quietly and unobtrusively.

It was against this background of Chartism that Mrs. Gaskell lived and moved. In the agitated scene her experiences were first-hand. Her work lay directly among her

husband's parishioners, and she was not slow in profiting
from her lesson. She saw ; she observed ; more than this,
she felt. Revelations which could not be conscientiously
ignored outraged by their factual truth. Contact with
homes, more often oozing dens, in which huddled whole
families forgotten by society and reduced to destitution by
unemployment for months at a stretch, was, to feeling
observers like herself at least, a shuddering experience.
Right up to the later 'forties conditions prevailed of savage
degradation. Squalid lives were patiently endured until
they, too, rotted to pieces from moral gangrene. Sometimes
the total income of a family averaged one shilling and
sixpence a week : where relief was obtained it was frequently
a shilling a head. The whole situation had developed at a
rush. Neither legislation nor organised philanthropy was
equal to a state of things which had transformed the country's
economy in the space of a few years. For in 1833, as Douglas
Jerrold had observed, nobody was thinking about the poor
and by 1839 nobody was thinking about anything else.

In Manchester, the heart of industrialism, the problem was
acute. The theme of *Mary Barton* is based on conditions
prevailing among the mill-hands and operatives throughout
the 'thirties : its purpose was to mediate between employers
and workpeople sore with injustices they could feel but
could not account for, and full of grievances they were
unable to remedy. From first to last it is a social novel,
with reform as its object ; one of the most effective, since
sincerity was its hall-mark.

To persuade the employers that the operatives had a case ;
to convince the operatives that the employers also had their
troubles : these were Mrs. Gaskell's immediate aims. She
set out to probe, to diagnose and to reveal ; not to remedy.

The action takes place during the unsettled 'thirties. A fluent opening shows her at her ease, introducing her chief characters as they walk across the fields in the spring.

> It was an early May evening—the April of the poets ; for heavy showers had fallen all the morning, and the round, soft, white clouds which were blown by a west wind over the dark blue sky, were sometimes varied by one blacker and more threatening. The softness of the day tempted forth the young green leaves, which almost visibly fluttered into life ; and the willows which that morning had had only a brown reflection in the water below, were now of that tender gray-green which blends so delicately with the spring harmony of colours.

In all rural description, and particularly of unspectacular scenes, Mrs. Gaskell never went wrong. Fields, footpaths, commons and cottages are all approached lyrically, and the opening paragraph is very characteristic :

> There are some fields near Manchester, well known to the inhabitants as " Green Heys Fields," through which runs a public footpath to a little village about two miles distant. In spite of these fields being flat, and low, nay, in spite of the want of wood . . . there is a charm about them which strikes even the inhabitant of a mountainous district, who sees and feels the effect of contrast in these commonplace but thoroughly rural fields, with the busy, bustling, manufacturing town he left but half an hour ago. Here and there an old black and white farm-house, with its rambling outbuildings, speaks of other times and other occupations than those which now absorb the population of the neighbourhood. Here in their seasons may be seen the country business of hay-making, ploughing . . .

It is easy to feel the effectiveness of this descriptive power. In this Mrs. Gaskell never falters. But thereafter, the whole, top-heavy story proceeds, now rushing, now stumbling along a succession of bewildering and improbable coincidences.

Apart from its sincerity and humanity, to read *Mary Barton* is to plunge into a world of melodrama.

It is not well constructed. Sentimentality cloys the characters, and turgid dialogue obscures their reality. Again and again occurs the unlikely event, until with unrelenting optimism the climax is reached with the highly melodramatic reappearance of the prostitute Esther who crawls out of her garish and teeming underworld to collapse, dying, beneath the windows of the Barton home. Humour, in this first novel of Mrs. Gaskell's, is not conspicuous. No work wrung from a tormented heart to draw attention to great social wrongs could be an outlet for that exquisitely smiling muse who fortunately later reasserted her influence.

As a thesis *Mary Barton* was indicative. It showed that through industrialism society had produced sub-human living conditions for two-thirds of its population and was either unable or unwilling to remedy the causes. Mrs. Gaskell's assumption was that society would be willing, if able. She finger-pointed very clearly the conclusions arrived at by the Manchester operatives that the employers were able, though unwilling. Her indications were clear and precise ; her vision unclouded by bigotry or prejudice. She was neither harsh nor narrow in her views. She had studied her subject at close range ; from the centre of the swaying battle. She reported truthfully, and was shocked at her own disclosures. As the wife of a minister she was drawn, a neutral, into the maelstrom of capital and labour, and from its still centre her dramatic gesture went forth.

Considered purely as a story and romance the affairs of Mary Barton and Jem Wilson are not of exceptional interest. The dominating factor is that of the gradual moral deterioration and decay of the powerfully drawn John Barton through

unemployment, domestic tragedy, near-starvation and con-
spiracy to murder and finally to death. His career could be
defined as an object-lesson in the waste of human effort
through misunderstanding. Yet compared with Felix Holt
there is a *naïveté* in the drawing of John Barton which
points to the influence of emotional sympathy in Mrs.
Gaskell, rather than to an intellectual understanding of a
forceful, dissatisfied nature.

It was chiefly in her lack of experience that she failed
to create in *Mary Barton* a work that would outlast her
generation. At the time it was topical and human. It was
generated by an intensity of sympathy. At the moment of
its appearance it was like touchwood to the fires of progress.
But when the flames subsided, if they left the whitened
bones of John Barton, as a stark lecture in anatomy, they
also left a bewildering tangle of prolixity. The book is by
no means a work of art. The plot is involved, the characters
too numerous, death-beds and anti-climaxes redundant.
Passages of power are remarkable throughout the crowded
scenes ; this is a strength in all Mrs. Gaskell's work, an
instinctive ability to handle dramatic effects which are a
feature of many of her novels. The fire at Carson's Mill
is described with understanding of crowd emotion and the
accuracy of an eye-witness. This is paralleled by the strike
at Thornton's factory in *North and South*, the animation of
the county balls in *Ruth* and *Wives and Daughters*, the
return of the whalers and the press-gang scenes in *Sylvia's
Lovers*. All these incidents are so vividly described that the
impression of personal experience is transmitted and evident.

What disturbs the very early work is the artificial dialogue,
the mawkishness of sentiment, the abundant coincidence,
the innumerable death-beds. Yet in its own day *Mary*

Barton rang true. Samuel Bamford, the Radical, in a letter to Mrs. Gaskell declared that " in describing the dwellings of the poor, their manners, their kindliness to each other, their feelings towards their superiors . . . you have been very faithful." It was in his opinion a mournfully beautiful production ; impossible to read with tearless eyes.

It is, indeed, a mournful story ; pessimism is its keynote. In the end Mary and Jem Wilson, after their numberless ordeals, resort to emigration. It was a defeatist solution : one that the aged Maria Edgeworth was quick to notice. In an exhaustively critical though admiring letter to Mary Holland [1] she claimed that it was no solution at all, since it avoided the issue and merely implied escape, not reform.

The profound impression created by *Mary Barton* is reflected in the prominence to which Mrs. Gaskell was suddenly raised by her contemporaries. Overnight she was deafened by acclamations, although she also met some hostility. There were two schools of opinion. Humanitarians welcomed her entry into the arena ; critics, like W. R. Greg, considered her book to be unjust and emotionally dangerous. In an article [2] Greg, whose local prestige was considerable, came forward in support of the employers, accusing Mrs. Gaskell of sentimentality, and the operatives of improvidence : a charge which she had never been concerned to defend. Being herself manifestly impartial, his criticism stuck. She was to return to the problem later and examine it, as it might have been, through the other end of the telescope.

Mrs. Gaskell, unlike Miss Martineau, was no intellectual philosopher. She lacked the powerful grasp of George Eliot,

[1] A cousin of Mrs. Gaskell's.
[2] *Mistaken Aims and Attainable Ideals of the Artisan class.*

the burning imagination of the Brontës. She, too, could create vividly, but her creations are of a lesser order : they proceed from knowledge and are limited to experience.

Yet the fairy who attended her christening had held in reserve for this favoured child a gift which had been denied her greater contemporaries. She endowed her with an immense understanding of the capacities of the human heart, and compassion for its shortcomings. She is the interpreter of the Christian ethic. She pleaded compassion and loving-kindness. In a word, she felt. Hers were sentiments which could be shared, expressed in language that could be understood.

Two dominant trends in her nature control in effect her literary work : a constant attempt at reconciliation between her natural escapism and the sense of moral obligation forced upon her by period, circumstances and upbringing.

From her father she inherited a taste for research, antiquarian in its tendencies. From her mother's stock came an intuitive feeling for the values of rural life and ways, crystallised in retrospect by Knutsford and the Cheshire locality. Largely her literary struggle appears to be an effort to reconcile the antiquarian with the social reformer. The result was a clash between her affection for past, and regard for present, conditions. And the reforming side of Mrs. Gaskell's nature did not always win the struggle. We read *Mary Barton* not for pleasure, but for the same reason that we take medicine : to effect a cure. But we can still read *My Lady Ludlow* with something approaching pure delight : for its subtle irony and delicate understanding, above all for its wit.

Mrs. Gaskell's nature was fundamentally happy. The serenity that could not be concealed created *Cranford*, *My*

Lady Ludlow, *Wives and Daughters*. Her moral indignation indeed flared up once again with *Ruth*, but after that it settled into the matronly armchair of gossip and romance. By the time *North and South* is reached the sting has been taken out of the industrial theme. It was, after all, her mission to mediate. To compose the differences between past and present, master and man, bigot and latitudinarian.

Throughout the third quarter of the nineteenth century *Mary Barton* was Mrs. Gaskell's chief title to fame. Emily Winkworth had been the first of their circle to suspect the authorship. She had, innocently enough, been discussing the book when all at once everybody turned suspiciously silent, and Mrs. Gaskell " suddenly popped down under the table to look for something which I'm sure wasn't there . . ." It was exquisitely, movingly written. It was upsetting to the emotions. In those days of earnest enthusiasm tears were no disgrace as Stephen Winkworth confirmed when he, too, had read the new novel. " With that and Mill," he wrote, " one would have a library. Only it makes me cry too much."

Mrs. Jameson was not even prepared to compare it with any contemporary work, for she had declared that since *The Bride of Lammermoor* nothing had appeared to equal *Mary Barton*.

" Paraclete of the Bartons," cried Landor in a burst of poetical admiration, " Pure and mighty, such art thou."

Yet here and there tastes were fastidious : extremes of approval were weighed. Mrs. Browning, for instance, was disappointed. There was power in it, she conceded, and truth, too. Yet when all was said and done she placed it in the class-book category.

IV

MRS. GASKELL was thirty-eight. Success had come to her after a crucial period ; what had remained of the " little giddy, thoughtless thing " who had taken on the esteemed minister of Cross Street Chapel ? She seems to have been, in character and appearance, the very ideal of mid-Victorianism. From contemporary description we see her clearly. The queenly presence, the broadly serene brow and classical features with their extraordinary mobility which were " constantly illuminated by a varying play of expression." A wonderful, doubtless an incessant, talker, her conversation is compared with the " gleaming ripple and rush of a clear, deep stream in sunshine." An atmosphere of ease and leisure enveloped her ; in her company time flew quickly by. Clearly she was vital, animated, entertaining. Her faculties as a story-teller assisted a remarkable memory and, apparently, a racy humour. " All so warmed and brightened by her sympathy and feeling that in her presence," says Catherine Winkworth, " her charm counted for more than her power."

There it was : she possessed the indefinable charm that attracted and captured so many entranced admirers. As a story-teller she is said to have been incomparable. Yet not everyone yielded to her spell. It would perhaps have been too conventional for the rebellious spirit of Miss Jewsbury, who observed in a letter to Mrs. Carlyle : " I have a notion that if one could get at the *Mary Barton* that is the kernel of

Mrs. Gaskell one would like her, but I never have done so
yet."

On the whole Mrs. Carlyle concurred ; when she stayed
with Mrs. Gaskell as she eventually did, she found her " a
very kind, cheery woman in her own house : but there is
an atmosphere of moral dullness about her as about all
Socinian women."

Here, cheery was the operative word, and Mrs. Carlyle
was well aware of it. What with her usual sub-acid scorn
she implied by moral dullness was a dig at Mrs. Gaskell's
powers of compromise. For there is no doubt she wished
to please. And she did please in spite of a critical minority.
But she could never entirely satisfy that contemptuous dis-
regard for conventional taste which Mrs. Carlyle flicked
about her like a lash.

For to oppose established opinions offended Mrs. Gaskell's
sense of fitness. She was always acutely sensitive to un-
friendly criticism. The courage which exposed social abuses
in spite of the dreaded counter-attacks was entirely lacking
when it came to flouting convention. And this element—a
regard for wordly considerations—meant certainly to Mrs.
Carlyle a limitation in development.

In no way was a certain lack of integrity more apparent
than in the pronounced relegation of her art to the lowest
rank in the household. Admittedly her family responsibilities were great. So were her external duties. Yet need
her domestic and social obligations have been given such an
abiding priority over writing ? Her domestic economy was
a boast, a matter for pride. Later, cows, pigs and poultry
were added. Cookery was a well-known feature of the
Gaskell *ménage*. These have vanished. The few books
remain. Yet we have not to-day the heart to echo that

evout comment, uttered it may be not wholly without a
ouch of irony by Miss Winkworth :

> Her books, indeed, were only written when all possible
> domestic and social claims had been satisfied.

Part of the novel was first submitted in MS. to William
Howitt, who, as her literary sponsor, had expressed interest
in her progress. While, according to Mrs. Browning, it
was being offered to nearly all the London publishers
before being finally accepted on John Forster's advice by
Chapman and Hall, Howitt had printed three short stories
by " Cotton Mather Mills, Esq." in the newly launched
Howitt's Journal.

The first of these, *Libbie Marsh's Three Eras*, is a story
of unselfishness in a Manchester court. An improving moral
coated with unexceptionable sentiments was to be drawn
therefrom.

The next, *The Sexton's Hero*, also on improvement bent,
showed another side to Mrs. Gaskell's work. Her natural
instinct for collecting traditional ancedotes in the places she
visited gave her a chance to exercise her considerable powers
of scenic description. Here, too, she used the occasion to
declare her principles. Pacifism is clearly displayed. As
with Edith Cavell three-quarters of a century later, so too
with her. Patriotism was not enough ; the highest form of
heroism could not be linked with destructive motives such
as that " poor unchristian heroism, whose manifestation
consists in injury to others."

Again and again in no uncertain terms does she assert
her convictions, affirm her faith and emphasise her belief
in the essential necessity : Christianity and the practice of
its teachings. As a liberal and a pacifist she was open-minded.

She believed in the power of example rather than in the force of punishment.

The third contribution to *Howitt's Journal* was a trifle *Christmas Storms and Sunshine*. It is facetious and garrulous, showing no artistry ; illustrating, rather, that utter lack of artistry in her early work, much of which is commonplace and prosaic, and chiefly remarkable for an excessive sentimentality. Only two qualities are as yet perceptible and they lie below the sugar-without-spice crust of uplifting Victorian sentiment. The first is her essential Christianity in the profoundest sense, with its emphatic insistence on the universal need for Charity. The second is her innate power of conveying atmosphere : indeed so marked is this power that her novels are impregnated from the opening passages with the effect she wishes to produce. Yet, in these early stories as in much of *Mary Barton*, the first quality is disguised in pietistic moralising of the goody type which gained, in some measure, a popularity with sentimental writers as the century advanced. The second, brief and inspired, appears so far only in intermittent flashes.

Mrs. Gaskell had seen relatively little of the world in the wider sense. Parochial festivities and social work were instructive if limiting slices of provincial life. Of contact with influential minds, and the limitless horizons of the outer world with its diversities of range, she had limited experience.

All this was now to change. After the uproar caused by *Mary Barton* she was by common consent a public figure. From the obscure duties of a Unitarian minister's wife in an industrial area, she suddenly found herself on terms with much that was brightest, wisest and most progressive in mid-Victorian England. Almost before she knew what she was doing she was in London breakfasting at Samuel

Roger's with Dickens and the Macreadys. Meeting Thackeray. Dining with clever Mr. Forster in his sumptuous chambers, and exacting a promise that he would write her a long, long letter pointing out all the weaknesses in *Mary Barton*. There was a visit to Hampton Court with Emily Winkworth ; there was sightseeing with Tom Taylor. A call, too, on Carlyle whose encomiums in a letter, recognising her opulence of soul, must have flattered to ruin a more sophisticated generation.

Another time at Monckton Milnes' there is a breakfast, to meet Guizot, F. D. Maurice, Archdeacon Hare and Ludlow. Politics and religion were soundly thrashed out, and practical philanthropy earnestly discussed. Meeting Froude in a railway carriage meant sound, grave talk ; but ever in the background over the speakers' shoulders are sounding clarion words : " Chartism," " Physical Force," " Education."

The exciting year closed with more hope than had been thought possible for some time past. In 1846 another child had been added to the family of girls, Julia Bradford. The ranks were closed. After this there were no more. But in the latter part of the year there was a new and this time a permanent removal to a fresh home. A large house was obtained : 42 Plymouth Grove, on the outskirts of Manchester, in the middle of a shrubbery and facing the fields frequented by dairy herds. It was to be the scene of triumph and prosperity. Its guests were to be frequent and well-entertained. Names begin to appear : names like Dickens, Carlyle, Ruskin, Martineau and Brontë assemble gradually under her roof.

In 1850 Dickens opened the year well for Mrs. Gaskell. He invited her to contribute to the inaugural number of

3

Household Words. To this request she submitted *Lizzie Leigh.* Unworthy of much comment—this story concerns a prodigal daughter ; its main argument is forgiveness, and through love, redemption. Sentimental treatment impairs the effect.

V

A FEW years earlier the appearance of *Jane Eyre* and the mystery surrounding its author had caused considerable speculation. Rumours had been widespread. Currer Bell, at pains to preserve anonymity, had by 1849 been compelled to discard the veil of secrecy : it was being torn away by enthusiasts, among whom was Mrs. Gaskell, passionately intrigued. Now the publication of *Shirley* decided her to dispense with formalities. She had addressed a letter with a copy of *Mary Barton* to the recluse of Haworth. A little later, and she was triumphantly writing to Miss Winkworth :

> Currer Bell (aha ! What will you give me for a secret ?) She's a she—that I will tell you—who has sent me *Shirley*.

The following summer Charlotte Brontë accepted an invitation from Sir James and Lady Kay-Shuttleworth to visit them at Briery Close. The Gaskells were also invited to complete the party. But Mr. Gaskell, espoused to Manchester and his sermons, declined. He was never easy to dislodge, as his wife had already discovered. She, however, accepted and went up to Windermere, reaching a pleasant house high above Low-wood after dark on a late August evening.

The drawing-room, entered suddenly, was at first a little dazzling, but when she recovered her sight she was being welcomed by her host and hostess, and a small person in black silk who after greeting the newcomer went silently on with her work. That evening was dedicated to mutual

35

observation, but the next day, after breakfast, the guests were taken out on to the lake by their host. Some tentatives were begun. Mrs. Gaskell described it all later, in detail :

" Miss Brontë agreed with me in liking Mr. Newman's *Soul*, and in liking *Modern Painters*, and the idea of the *Seven Lamps* ; and she told me about Father Newman's lectures at the Oratory in a very quiet, concise, graphic way."

The effects of suffering, too, were very marked.

" Suffering enough to have taken out every spark of merriment, and to be shy and silent from the habit of extreme, intense solitude. Such a life as Miss Brontë's I never heard of before."

Is this the present anticipating the future ? Certain moments in Mrs. Gaskell's life seem to be lit with pre-monitory instinct. This was one such moment. It was also the hesitating prelude to a rather curious friendship. That constitutional timidity of Charlotte Brontë's needed a persuasive method of cultivation. Mrs. Gaskell had that method. And temperamentally they were both opposites. Her own nature, sunny, open, perhaps rather obvious, was so uninhibited as to possess a disarming attractiveness. Gradually she succeeded in breaking down the walls of suspicion that enclosed her new acquaintance. And the following year Miss Brontë arrived in Manchester on a short visit to Plymouth Grove.

During this period a few short stories made their appearance in *Household Words* : *Lizzie Leigh*, *The Well of Pen-Morfa* and *The Heart of John Middleton* were all published during 1850, towards the end of which came a Christmas book, under the imprint of Chapman & Hall, *The Moorland Cottage*, appropriately illustrated by Birkett

Foster, with whose vignettes the story has an analogous charm. Here life is a frosted Christmas card, its effect tender, fragile and sentimental. At times it irritates taste and offends judgment, it is never less than pretty. Its style is simple, and the initial dialogue between the two small children an example of Mrs. Gaskell's lifelong fluctuations between fidelity to nature and compromise with convention.

This scene, in which false sentiment is exploded, is an early instance of those remarkable flashes of intuition which play here and there over Mrs. Gaskell's later work like summer lightning. Without comment two children are intimately revealed in their innermost thoughts. Just for a few moments they are children reacting sincerely, unfettered by prejudice, heartless in their virgin indifference to sorrow, only conscious of the dread of being conspicuous.

But, after this, as so often, Mrs. Gaskell loses courage and retreats into unexceptionable sentiment.

In *The Moorland Cottage* several types are put through their paces for later and fuller performances. Nancy the maid, shrewd and loving, forgoes her wages in the hour of distress, just as Sally comes to the rescue in *Ruth* ; Martha in *Cranford* ; Dixon in *North and South* ; Kester in *Sylvia's Lovers* ; Dixon again, less obviously in *A Dark Night's Work*. The close association between master and servant, obligation and devotion, is a marked feature in most of Mrs. Gaskell's work. The gestures in themselves range from the touching to the moving. They form a strong supporting argument to her plea for the co-operation of the classes, for the interchange of mutual affection and trust.

Of the other characters, Mrs. Buxton is a preliminary sketch for the delicate Mrs. Hamley of *Wives and Daughters* ; Edward Browne reappears in many forms as a prodigal

weakling ; Maggie, inspiring prototype of her more famous
namesake, Maggie Tulliver, has many of the characteristics
of Molly Gibson, particularly her warmth and sincerity ;
Mrs. Browne contains a hint of that consummation of dis-
content, Clare, in *Wives and Daughters* ; she is, however,
less good-natured, though as pettish, as pretentious.

Throughout Mrs. Gaskell's work there is always a tendency
for her plots to verge upon bankruptcy. Harping upon
certain themes, a repetition, not always very varied, of
characters and circumstances, seems constantly to provoke
similarity of action as the same circumstances arise. This
results in a certain monotony. The stories echo with
recurring themes ; situations, principally autobiographical,
are regularly repeated since she lacked the originality of
absolute creativeness. Allusions to infants, abandoned, dying
or in peril ; to young men vanishing at sea ; to old retainers
coming to the rescue with their life's savings in the hour of
their employer's need are so numerous that a few instances
will be sufficient for reference. The motherly instinct in
Mrs. Gaskell was immense. Maternal love and care is given
great prominence. The death of the twins in *Mary Barton*
is poignant. The long journey by coach of Job Legh with
the baby was suggested by her own removal to Knutsford
after the death of her mother. In *Cranford* the Signora
Brunoni gives an exhaustive account of hairbreadth
escapes, carrying her baby through the Indian jungle. In
Lizzie Leigh mother love is, in a twofold case, the
dominating theme. Mrs. Leigh devotes herself to finding
her daughter : Lizzie's illegitimate child dies " a little
unconscious sacrifice to reclaim her wandering mother."
So, as in *Ruth*, the child of shame becomes the instrument
of redemption.

Mysterious disappearance is another repeated theme. Partly on its own account, but also because it provided an escape for inconvenient characters which could always be recalled by a stroke of the pen at the end of the story. Will Wilson in *Mary Barton*, Frederick in *North and South*, Poor Peter in *Cranford* and, variously, both Charley Kinraid and Philip Hepburn in *Sylvia's Lovers* are all lost sight of over a stretch of years though they return to civilisation when required to complete the story. Holdsworth of *Cousin Phillis* escapes to Canada ; Roger Hamley of *Wives and Daughters* goes out to Africa, and though neither of these actually disappears, each fulfils a particular function by his absence.

Finally, the article *Disappearances*, published in *Household Words*, 1851, explored various cases akin to that of John Stevenson, who in 1827 had sailed to India and, in spite of a rumour that he had landed at Calcutta, was never heard of again.

But on every occasion that Mrs. Gaskell indulges in subjects involving the extraordinary, the inexplicable or the marvellous, there is a careless abandonment of historical accuracy in favour of purely sensational effect. The good-wife in her nature was sometimes stronger than the student.

An interest in legends, ghost stories and supernatural manifestations as a whole is apparent throughout much of her work. Many of her magazine stories reflect this facility for thrilling the reader to the detriment of her best work which certainly suffered in consequence. But as a corollary to this interest she made use, in some of her novels, of much local superstition and folk-lore which is introduced here and there, notably in *Mary Barton* and *Ruth*. The latter work abounds in allusions to certain occurrences and their unlucky

consequences. Mrs. Morgan, of the Inn, discusses Bellingham's chances of recovery in characteristic terms :

> " Mr Jones said to-night was a turning-point ; but I doubt it,
> for it is four days since he was taken ill, and whoever heard of
> a sick person taking a turn in an even number of days ? It's
> always on the third, or fifth, or seventh, or so on. . . . I don't
> think he will get better myself, though—Gelert does not howl
> for nothing."

Here two superstitions are associated in one connection.
Similarly, in *Mary Barton*, Alice Wilson in an attempt to
speed the parting soul of the second twin attempts to separate
it from its mother, for,

> ". . . He cannot die while she's wishing him."
> " Wishing him ? " said Mary, in a tone of inquiry.
> " Ay ; donno' ye know what ' wishing ' means ? There's
> none can die in the arms of those who are wishing them sore
> to stay on earth. The soul o' them as holds them won't let the
> dying soul go free ; so it has a hard struggle for the quiet of
> death. . . ."

In *Ruth* foxgloves are thought to have " knowledge,"
bowing their heads at the passing by of a spirit. Shooting
stars are unlucky. So is the dog-rose : " Never form any
plan while sitting near one for it will never answer."

This had also been alluded to in her letter to Mary Howitt
years before, accounting for her failure in the first literary
adventure.[1]

In *Ruth* also ill-luck is believed for a baby if tears fall on
its face before it is weaned ; while a death in the home is
forecast at the swarming of bees.

In *Cranford* the sewing of two pieces of old flannel in the
shape of a cross on an inner garment is held to be a protection
against danger.

[1] *Sketches Among the Poor.*

There are other favourite themes. In most of her novels a crisis arises in the affairs of the principal family entailing financial loss or eventual ruin. This necessitates the devoted gesture of a faithful servant : wages are sacrificed ; teapot and savings bank yield their hoards ; mistress and maid continue together in reduced contentment. We see Martha and Miss Matty ; Dixon and Margaret Hale ; Kester and the Robsons ; Sally and the Bensons. Dixon in *A Dark Night's Work* stands his trial for murder rather than accuse the memory of Mr. Wilkins. Although all these events fall naturally into place in their respective stories, they are, nevertheless, recurring situations proving a versatile but not wholly original artist.

VI

CONSIDERING her creative limits it is the more remarkable that suddenly and with no apparent effort Mrs. Gaskell's originality flowered in a work which no one else could have written, and which has never since been either contested or imitated.

Soundings, it is true, had already been taken. In *Mr. Harrison's Confessions*, a short story written a few months earlier for *The Ladies' Companion*, she had experimented playfully with the hilarious narrative of a newly arrived young doctor in a little town in the Knutsford setting. His adventures among the inhabitants on setting up his practice are described with overflowing high spirits ; types are introduced which, with different characters and other names, are later to become so familiar. They are all there : the doctors in riding boots, the mittened spinsters, the pair of sisters, dominating and submissive without whom no Knutsford story is authentic. The Misses Parkinson anticipate the Misses Jenkyns by only a few months. They are of the same quality but of inferior art. They do not inspire affection. However, they fulfil their role. The senior lady, more gaunt and masculine than Miss Debōrah Jenkyns, has the same protective attitude toward the younger Miss Caroline. But then Miss Caroline is no Miss Matty. She has in fact some unpleasing aspects : one of these is disloyalty to her sister. There is also the indispensable busybody. Miss Horsman's ill-nature is more pronounced than that of Miss Pole : hers is altogether a more spiteful and vindictive character.

It was in this type of story that Mrs. Gaskell excelled. Her lightness of touch, shrewdness of observation and tolerance of outlook acted like a blessing on the absurdities of human nature. The mood suited her ; like a cat she purred contentedly. All at once and quite unconsciously she came to her involuntary masterpiece.

Cranford originated as a single sketch for *Household Words,* was prolonged into a series in answer to requests for more and was subsequently published as a book.

Cranford is Mrs. Gaskell's homage to the country town of her youth. It is really no more than a collection of papers founded upon people and events she could remember at Knutsford. There is no attempt at either plot or story, merely a roughly connected string of irrelevant incidents in the lives of some elderly ladies. Its charm is that their lives are so uneventful. The very fact that their circumstances are straitened and their existences so placid lends interest to their gallant struggles to preserve that elegant economy upon which Cranford standards were so justly based.

It is the perfect judgment with which these sketches are written that has made them one of the minor English classics : it is this which has placed Mrs. Gaskell among the lasting English writers.

For at least two decades after her death she was popularly identified as " the author of *Mary Barton.*" Three generations later, by a process of readjustment, she is established for good as the author of *Cranford.* It is no matter for surprise ; causes and crusades long since won, were, in the 'fifties and 'sixties, still painfully inflaming thorns in the plump Victorian flesh. Once removed there was little of intrinsic merit to give permanence to the book itself. The case of *Cranford* operates in reverse. Its value lies in the very perfection with

which former English customs and ways are presented and
preserved. Precisely because the basic virtues of rural life
are so abiding an attraction the appeal of *Cranford* is strongest
at a time when the past seems daily more precious, its
standards more regretted, its leisure more desirable.

But if Mrs. Gaskell is chiefly remembered as the creator
of immortal spinsters in an immemorial village it is also
true that *Cranford* has helped to sow in the popular fancy
the seeds of a false interpretation of parochial life. Through
no fault of Mrs. Gaskell's a country grateful for the per-
petuation of Miss Matty has commemorated her by the
self-conscious cult of the olde-worlde village. For this
doubtful benefit with all its attendant gentility : poke-bonnet
signs, copper kettles, oak settles, dimity ladies and dainty
teas we have partly to thank *Cranford* and Mrs. Gaskell.
For she it was who first made the English village aware of
itself as an object of interest. From this awareness it was only
a short step to commercialisation. It was she who, while
growing up in its heart, recognised a way of life that was
dying out. She whose idea it was to record that way of
life before it should be entirely obliterated by the rising new
industrial order.

Cranford in style and method is a continuation of the
manner begun in *Mr. Harrison's Confessions.* Gaiety is
in every line, but it is quiet, there is no effervescence ;
mature humour runs through the book, yet is never obvious,
and so obliquely presented that the characters appear amusing
because heightened by the naïve, almost detached participa-
tion of the narrator. Mary Smith, like Margaret Dawson in
My Lady Ludlow, never allows her personality to obtrude.
She is always the outsider, ready, if needed, to be useful ;
to retire if the effect can be heightened thereby.

Mrs. Gaskell, rarely enterprising where names are concerned, shines luminously through this personality. It is her
tact, her observation, her delicacy and her loving appreciation of absurdities which have made *Cranford*—alas !—
synonymous with the quaint. She eats peas off her knife
at the boorish Mr. Holbrook's, just as Mrs. Gaskell herself
once ate a nauseous decoction in a Cumberland farmhouse
to spare her hostess's feelings.

Although the effect of *Cranford* has been to play a part in
sentimentalising the idea of the little old-fashioned country
town, its general character is by no means over-sentimental,
full of feeling though it always is. For it is a masterpiece of
deliberate understatement. It is kindly, truthful and of a
humour that smiles with, as well as at, its subject. The
residents of a provincial backwater over a century ago, their
prejudices, their loyalties and their overwhelming self-
sufficiency are described with the delicacy of taste and
sympathy of feeling that have given it everywhere its
tremendous appeal. It is a fine work of art, standing alone
among the rest of Mrs. Gaskell's writing on account of the
perfection with which she recreated a facet of English life
which, though having disappeared in many outer aspects,
still retains certain of the recognisable spiritual qualities
which give it permanence. Not only is it still read on
account of its economy of style and restrained humour,
but because of its strong undertone of respect for the
endeavour of humanity to keep up its morale in spite of
circumstances.

For subdued irony, often employed with devastating effect,
it is a model of the craft which Mrs. Gaskell had suddenly
come to perfect. The best examples usually fall to Mary
Smith, who, in her character of impartial observer, is best able

to display it, as, for example, when she describes the contents of her letter :

> My father's was just a man's letter ; I mean it was very dull . . .

Again there is in timid Miss Matty's excitement at dining at Mr. Holbrook's, another example of that humour which broadly infuses the whole book like an adorable smile : " It is," she observes with her gentle diffidence, " so very pleasant dining with a bachelor. I only hope it is not improper, so many pleasant things are."

But if Miss Matty's simplicity is rare to-day, Miss Pole is still among us :

> Miss Pole was always the person, in the trio of Cranford ladies now assembled, to have had adventures. She was in the habit of spending the morning in rambling from shop to shop, not to purchase anything (except an occasional reel of cotton or a piece of tape), but to see the new articles and report upon them, and to collect all the stray pieces of intelligence in the town. She had a way, too, of demurely popping hither and thither into all sorts of places to gratify her curiosity on any point—a way which, if she had not looked so very genteel and prim, might have been considered impertinent. And now, by the expressive way in which she cleared her throat, and waited for all minor subjects (such as caps and turbans) to be cleared off the course, we knew she had something very particular to relate, when the due pause came.

The very fact that she never intended to prolong the *Cranford* episodes beyond the first two chapters, in which Miss Jenkyns and Captain Brown are disposed of ; the very unpremeditated nature of the resuscitated sequel is, more than anything else, a testimony to Mrs. Gaskell's extraordinary powers of improvisation. Had it not been that Dickens was so pleased with the first instalment, and that the characters immediately assumed an individual significance for so many people, nothing might have been heard of the tale again. But there was a general demand for a continuation : Ruskin, with characteristic emphasis, " flew into a passion at Captain Brown being killed, and would not go any further."

Of the Knutsford residents reputed to have been in her mind as the various originals, many were identified. Not so, however, by the prudent author. Mrs. Gaskell took care to admit of no conscious originals of her characters. Perhaps, considering her reputation for indiscretion, it was as well.

Apart from the highly individual *Cranford* manner she was not original in her narrative prose. She wrote and thought conventionally, expressing herself frequently by the familiar process of repetition, and in the earlier work clichés are prominent, the formula too often readily produced. Adjectives are frequent : in the earlier stories hardly a sentence would not be improved without them ; they weaken by their commonplace quality. With progress, restraint begins to be noticeable in this respect ; adjectives become rarer, but to the last they retain a tendency to be commonplace.

It is the same with names. Pedestrianism infects her every choice with Wordsworthian sobriety. For these she either cared nothing, or else totally lacked imagination. As with her stock list of characters so with her stock nomenclature : names like Dawson, Barton, Benson and Gibson recur throughout her work. Ordinary everyday names like Mary Smith and Maggie Browne. Even these have to be repeated. There are two Molly Gibsons, one keeps a sweet-shop in *Mary Barton* ; there are two Dixons, the maid in *North and South*, the gardener in *A Dark Night's Work*. Even the glamour of a highwayman is a little tarnished by the name

of Higgins ; as for the *Cranford* doctor he is called Hoggins
—which, however, does not prevent the democratic Lady
Glenmire from recognising his many virtues. This is all a
great triumph of the ordinary. It seems never to have
attracted comment yet would appear to reflect something of
the implied worthiness noted by Mrs. Carlyle. Yet here and
there Mrs. Gaskell takes a surprising departure from her
ordinary names. *Sylvia's Lovers* contains a more original
collection than most of the earlier books, Charley Kinraid
and Philip Hepburn both break away from the usual convention ; and in *Wives and Daughters* new ground is broken,
the egregious Hyacinth Clare has a name which, in the
'sixties, must have verged on the improbable.

Names in a story are after all of some importance. A
well found name can reinforce a character ; above all it
must convince. It must fit its wearer like an individual
garment. Exotic or facetious names, the grotesques of
Dickens excepted, are another matter altogether. George
Eliot, whose very choice revealed her intellectual boldness,
understood this as well as any novelist before or since her
time. Names like Glegg and Tulliver give complexion to
her characters, Adam Bede and Silas Marner are complete,
Mrs. Transome conveys a whole era and a class.

Mrs. Gaskell's imaginative weakness is shown up by the
poverty of her names : they are dull ; they are like mass-
produced clothes, designed for everybody they fit no one.

Yet with all her superficial defects she was a born story-
teller. She knew exactly what effect she wished to obtain,
and she obtained it without apparent effort. Here and there
she appears to lose grip of her plot, a tendency most apparent
toward the close of *Wives and Daughters*, while a definite
loss of interest is obvious at the end of *Sylvia's Lovers*. Yet

on the whole, judging from what is known of the position to which her work was relegated in her household, the wonder is that, like Dr. Johnson's dog walking on its hind legs, it was done at all, that she accomplished so much, so well and with so little apparent effort.

She wrote at the dining-room table at Plymouth Grove, after breakfast was cleared away and while daughters skipped in and out of the room, talking, planning, discussing arrangements all together. Instructions were required by maids about meals, by the gardener about fruit, a dress-maker wished to fit a skirt or Meta needed advice about a sketch. Bonnets had to be trimmed, and headaches had a tiresome persistence throughout, which was perhaps not surprising. Privacy at all events was undreamed of.

Later, in Paris, conditions were rather more irresponsible and amusing, but still less conducive to concentration. *Wives and Daughters* was mostly written on the mantelpiece of Mme. Mohl's drawing-room, to the accompanying musketry rattle of Mme. Mohl's chaff.

VII

IN 1853 Mrs. Gaskell paid a late September visit to Haworth. Her impressions were vivid. Remote moors, brown with blighted heather, rolled upward and away from the precipitous village. In the Parsonage silence smothered the remaining embers of life and genius. Mr. Brontë was seventy-six, Tabby nearing ninety and Charlotte already in her thirty-eighth year.

The visit appears to have brought the two women nearer than their earlier meetings. For one thing, Charlotte on home ground was, possibly, less timid than when enduring society away. At any rate confidences were more fully exchanged : a mutual sympathy can be detected in their developing correspondence. Sincerity, on one hand, at any rate, compensated for more than a hundred compliments. Charlotte Brontë, pessimistic as ever, yet adamant in her intellectual honesty, had perceived very clearly the lack in Mrs. Gaskell of absolute artistic integrity, so essential an element in herself. It was after this realisation that, partly puzzled, partly distressed, she wrote her mind in an unforgettable letter :

A thought strikes me. Do you, who have so many friends, so large a circle of acquaintance—find it easy, when you sit down to write, to isolate yourself from all those ties, and their sweet associations, so as to be your *own woman*, uninfluenced or swayed by the consciousness of how your work may affect other minds ; what blame or what sympathy it may call forth ? Does no luminous cloud ever come between you and the severe Truth, as you know it in your own secret and clear-seeing soul ? In a word, are you never tempted to make your characters more amiable than the life, by the inclination to assimilate your thoughts to the thoughts of those who always *feel* kindly, but sometimes fail to *see* justly ? Don't answer the question ; it is not intended to be answered. . . .

Miss Brontë needed no reply. She knew. It was to her that the year before Mrs. Gaskell had outlined the proposed new novel that was materialising in her mind, just as *Villette* was developing in her own. They had exchanged comments and opinions. *Villette*, a shy bird, engaged to defer publication until after *Ruth* should have appeared. It was finally published in January 1853.

Mary Barton had been unequal and immature, its success depending more on the courage and sincerity which impelled it than on its literary merit. *Ruth* is another matter altogether. It is still the product of indignation and sympathy, but the writer comes forward sure of balance, judgment and materials. She dares to touch strings previously dormant, and sends them vibrating through the heart.

In substance *Ruth* turns on the subject of illegitimacy, and the problem of the unmarried mother. The story is a plea for a more charitable attitude by the righteous toward the victims of youthful error.

An orphan, seduced and abandoned, is eventually succoured by the Christ-like dissenter, Thurstan Benson, who, with his sister, makes a home for her. Here she has her baby. To cover her disgrace the Bensons contrive to pass her off as a widow, convinced that their purpose justifies the deception, that Ruth will, in time, be able to redeem her fault by honest living and by working to support her child.

Her past betrays her. Her seducer reappears, an unlaid ghost, and she and the Bensons are boycotted by a respectable Pharisee, a Mr. Bradshaw.

Atonement is the only way out. Ruth redeems herself
through sacrifice, nursing the victims of a typhus epidemic
of which she dies. The story has the same sincerity as
Mary Barton, enhanced not only by the pathos of the situation
but by a great increase in the power of writing. Though
technically still poor, and without much ability to develop
a plot, it is abundantly rich in creative feeling and characterisation. Infinite compassion pervades the whole. In
Thurstan Benson, Christianity, as revealed by its Founder, is
opposed to the conventional Christianity of Mr. Bradshaw,
the leading member of the congregation. The characters
are thus finely balanced, and delicately observed. The
purse-proud aggressiveness of Mr. Bradshaw, who " thinks
he can pay for ungracious speeches by a present," is one
of the most convincing examples of Mrs. Gaskell's war on
materialism. The impulsive warmth of his daughter
Jemima, the practical kindness of Faith Benson and the
strong humour of old Sally the maid are considerable
advances in her literary power. All of them surround the
central figure, the Magdalen Ruth, whose moral qualities
glorify her tragic circumstances.

Yet one cannot help wishing that Mrs. Gaskell had made
Ruth a little more human. There is, about this nearly
sublime figure, a passiveness which makes it negative. All
assurances of beauty and refinement leave one a little
unconvinced, a trifle incredulous. Herself a victim and the
creature of circumstance, she is really the motivating force
of the other characters. In fact, her case is the whole
thing : her personality is clouded, almost boring. Thus the
virtue with which Mrs. Gaskell sought to clothe her hangs
to-day a little lifeless, like drapery upon a lay figure.

Perhaps the only real failure in type is in the child

Leonard. He conveys no sense of reality at all, and seems not even a real child but a neurotic little prig, stuffed with sawdust. Mrs. Gaskell understood little girls far better. The Bradshaw daughters are natural and unforced. But then she had daughters of her own, while the loss of her son in infancy preyed rather morbidly upon her imagination.

Apart from Thurstan Benson the most striking character is that of Sally ; the prototype of all the future servants in the incomparable Gaskell collection. She is never surpassed even in the later books. Quotation is of little illustrative avail. The effect is obtained cumulatively and garrulously. All the shrewdness and pith in the North-country character, all its steadfastness and humour are brought together in these remarkable creations.

Time has partly supported George Eliot's opinion that *Ruth* would not prove to be an enduring or classical fiction. Along with her other reforming novels Mrs. Gaskell gave more thought to its immediate purpose than to the technical artistry of her performance. The purpose was achieved largely through her efforts ; the problem to-day is rather an individual one. The undergrowth she cleared with such courage and pain has been worn into a path by a procession of subsequent novelists. There is, too, an element of didactic pietism in this class of Mrs. Gaskell's work which becomes a little tiresome in the long run, however efficacious in a topical subject. Gently veiled as this usually is it is a familiar tendency in her earlier writing, as if the moral issue alone were insufficient.

At any rate the world dislikes its pills unsugared—in this case unsalted, unless they are tactfully administered. The unmarried mother, hounded by her fellows, stigmatised through her child and sitting in sackcloth to the end of her

days was a figure calculated to rouse all Mrs. Gaskell's sense
of compassion. But in this her essential motive was illogically
supported. There would have been no need for redemption
had she proved her argument for rehabilitation, which was
evidently the original intention. This, indeed, is the crown-
ing weakness, and Greg, her old antagonist, leapt at the
opportunity. In *The False Morality of Lady Novelists* he
exposed the flaw in logic. If Mrs. Gaskell meant to castigate
respectable society for cold-shouldering erring young women,
she should not have placed Ruth permanently on the stool
of repentance. She should never have forced her into a
redemptive death for lack of courage to rehabilitate her.

Alas ! for Mrs. Gaskell. Strictures on the immorality of
Ruth were innumerable and pronounced. Denunciations
poured in. Two of her Chapel neighbours, both fathers,
burnt the final volume in protest, a third forbade his wife
to read it. Cobden, an admirer, wrote apprehensively of
public censure : *Ruth* would be " considered dangerous
company for unmarried females even in a book." And so
it was. Yet the reason is to-day obscure. Never did
tempter appear in less attractive guise than as Bellingham ;
a young man in whom weakness, snobbishness, egotism and
vanity form the chief elements in his thoroughly unprincipled
nature. A young man by whom none but the shallowest
ignoramus would be deceived, and then not for long. He
is one of a stock list of profligates which was kept up Mrs.
Gaskell's sleeve for the purpose of tempting lovely women
to stoop to folly. Young Carson in *Mary Barton*, Bellingham and young Bradshaw in *Ruth*, Edward Browne in
The Moorland Cottage, Mr. Preston in *Wives and Daughters*,
Holdsworth in *Cousin Phillis* and Kinraid in *Sylvia's Lovers*
are to a certain extent all related, either by weakness and

dishonesty, or faithlessness and deceit, though both Holdsworth and Kinraid are more virile types and lack the calcu-
lating indecision of the rest. Osborne Hamley in *Wives and
Daughters* has just missed coming into the same category.
He begins with the familiar characteristics, but, mainly
through his brother's exertions, is morally shored up until
his premature death. In the main, fraud, deception and
moral cowardice are the prevailing characteristics of all
Mrs. Gaskell's bad young gentlemen. This is in fact about
the lowest depth of wickedness that she cares to depict. She
is unwilling to admit more evil types. She draws a line and
limits her world. With one exception, that of M. de la
Tourelle in *The Grey Woman*, she is incapable of creating an
unregenerate character.

But within the limits she set herself, superb examples begin
to appear of succinct analysis and fine observation. Young
Richard Bradshaw, child of a Pharisee, without his strength,
has learned, we read, to sprinkle his conversation with

> set sentences of goodness, which were like the flowers that
> children stick in the ground, and that have not sprung upwards
> from roots—deep down in the hidden life and experience of
> the heart.

Mrs. Gaskell that year was in a " quiver of pain." At all
times sensitive, less perhaps concerning questions of ability
than those of taste, she gave way to self-pity before the
adverse criticism of *Ruth*, comparing herself to " St. Sebastian
tied to a tree to be shot at with arrows." It was a foretaste
of future experience.

Another and at first a rather contradictory aspect of her
moral philosophy is to be found in her attitude toward
falsehood. Lies and their consequences play a definite part
in the moral aspect of her work, but lying for its own

sake and a deliberate analysis of its motives is constantly
enlarged on, is not necessarily followed by retribution and
is treated objectively and psychologically.

The clearest example occurs in *Ruth* when the Minister's
sister, Faith Benson, an exemplary character, goes out of her
way to elaborate the circumlocution she and her brother have
already agreed upon regarding Ruth's origins. She deliberately enjoys the proceeding. Having invented a fictitious
deceased husband for Ruth she decides him to have been a
surgeon, and defiantly defends her invention to her brother:

> " I do think I've a talent for fiction, it is so pleasant to invent,
> and make the incidents dovetail together ; and after all, if we
> are to tell a lie, we may as well do it thoroughly, or else it's of
> no use. A bungling lie would be worse than useless. And,
> Thurstan—it may be very wrong—but I believe—I am afraid
> I enjoy not being fettered by truth. Don't look so grave. You
> know it is necessary, if ever it was, to tell falsehoods now ; and
> don't be angry with me because I do it well."

That the effects of the Benson lie are ultimately catastrophic
is morally certain. What makes the interest is the careful,
extraordinarily subtle understanding of the psychology of
conscience operating in both the case of the benevolently
idealistic brother, as in that of his equally benevolent, more
practical sister.

Moreover, it is not denied that lying has an inventive
attraction of its own, and Mrs. Gaskell goes even further
than this when she excuses prevarication in the child,
Leonard. The Benson household,

> whose hearts were pained by this apparent unconsciousness of
> the difference between truth and falsehood, were unaccustomed
> to children, or they would have recognised this as a stage
> through which most infants, who would have lively imagina-
> tions, pass. . . .

Lying is therefore not so much the prerogative of the unregenerate as the indulgence of lively imaginations. The importance of telling the truth is of course never minimised, nor the consequences of its failure ignored. Yet the impression received, if not one of moral justification, comes occasionally very near to being so. In *North and South* Margaret Hale, for instance, denies having been at the station with her brother, and thus temporarily loses the respect of her lover ; but since the lie was the means of saving Frederick from unjust arrest her step is justified.

And Cynthia in *Wives and Daughters* is the agent for at least one illuminating remark, when she says to Molly :

> "Don't be so pedantically truthful. I never consider myself bound to be truthful, so I beg we may be on equal terms."

As for the veracity of Clare, nobody would dream of expecting it.

VIII

THE succeeding years were eventful. Visits to London, Paris and Normandy in 1853 and 1854 provided new friends and furnished new ideas. Miscellaneous contributions, short stories and *belles-lettres* appeared in *Household Words* over this period, and in the autumn of 1854 a new novel, conceived during the course of the year, was composed in leisure at Lea Hurst, the home of Florence Nightingale's family. Mrs. Gaskell, who had come to know that remarkable woman in London, had been invited by her parents to stay with them and work at her novel in peace. It was the eve of the departure for the Crimea ; absent or present, Miss Nightingale and her personality were all-pervading. The atmosphere of the entire household was charged with her intense spiritual and intellectual activity.

> She seems (writes Mrs. Gaskell to Catherine Winkworth) almost too holy to be talked about as a mere wonder. Mrs. Nightingale says, with tears in her eyes . . . that they are ducks and have hatched a wild swan. She seems as completely led by God as Joan of Arc.

Exalted by her surroundings Mrs. Gaskell set to work upon *North and South* in the sanctuary of the nurseries that had reared the wild swan and her sister ; the high nurseries overlooking an undulating park set in the wild wooded Derbyshire landscape. After six o'clock, when tea had been brought, she locked herself into her turreted solitude. There, stocked up with candles and coals, in the infinite silence of the large house, she set herself to decide upon the exact relations between Margaret Hale and John Thornton. When finished, the story, which had appeared serially throughout the winter of 1854, was published in two volumes by Chapman & Hall in 1855.

North and South, with its marked increase in power, discipline and probability is the last of Mrs. Gaskell's attempts to offer social problems to the world. By this time the interest of human relationships, the clash of wills and the perversities of character are matters which come more readily to her genius than the efforts at mediation which compassion and indignation had formerly aroused.

North and South is the opposite number to *Mary Barton*. It raises the employer's problems, for it was devised partly as a reply to those who, like W. R. Greg, had complained of biased views in the first novel. All the same its social issues are not the whole : while only the student can work up an interest in *Mary Barton* to-day, *North and South* is a book to be read for pleasure and for its own story. Gone is the cloying pathos which disfigures so much of the former book, and much, too, of most of the tales of working-class distress. Here there is no straining after effect. With the exception of the Higgins family, who are in the authentic *Mary Barton* tradition, the characters are strong, wilful, faithfully drawn. The social problem at the heart of the story is never allowed to swamp the human conflict ; the struggle of wills is the motivating force in the relationship of John Thornton, the man of granite, and the girl he had idealised. And Margaret Hale, though not a type to have much popular appeal, is the most arresting of Mrs. Gaskell's heroines. It is true that she lacks the charm of Molly Gibson's ingenuity, that the wayward temperament of Sylvia is also missing. All the same, she has a compelling power only

exacted by natures cast in generous lines : passionate, unexpected, didactic and grand. She dominates the book.
She stamps its whole character with her maddening and
inordinate pride. She is compounded of contradictory
elements. Tragedy is in her nature, so are exaltation and
devotion. Her religious convictions are intensely felt. With
a character like hers they make her intolerant, somewhat
prejudiced. She has little humour, and more often than not
it expresses itself in a snobbish sarcasm which is one of the
less desirable attributes of educated young ladyism in the
nineteenth century.

" What in the world do manufacturers want with the
classics or literature or the accomplishments of a gentle-
man ? " she cries out in contemptuous antipathy of Thornton
who stands for all she must either hate and hurt, or else
admire and adore.

Margaret Hale, a character admitting of no half-measures,
is by her very dramatic possibilities an example of the
versatility of Mrs. Gaskell's art. No resident of Cranford
would have known what to make of this magnificent creature
with her superb movements, her imperious manner, which,
at times frigid and aloof, accentuates her unspeakable pride.
Yet these Zenobia airs only enhance her more captivating
side. Her moods are of sudden emotion, impulsive generosity, languors, melting tendernesses. Her whole strong
nature, with its capacity for the uttermost limits of feeling,
fears always exposure to humiliation, and finally, but only
finally, yields to the irresistible sweep of its love. All these
are qualities which elevate. She has something Hardyesque,
an element lacking in more commonplace heroines. A
nobility of soul which, clashing with its destiny, is one of
Mrs. Gaskell's deeper achievements. This portrait of

Margaret is enough to strike all but the most lymphatic
readers :

> She stood by the table, not offering to sit down. Her eyelids
> were dropped half over her eyes ; her teeth were shut, not
> compressed ; her lips were just parted over them, allowing the
> white line to be seen between their curve. Her slow deep
> breathings dilated her thin and beautiful nostrils ; it was the
> only motion visible on her countenance. The fine-grained
> skin, the oval cheek, the rich outline of her mouth, its corners
> deep set in dimples—were all wan and pale to-day ; the loss
> of their usual natural healthy colour being made more evident
> by the heavy shadow of the dark hair, brought down upon her
> temples, to hide all sign of the blow she had received. Her
> head, for all its drooping eyes, was thrown a little back, in the
> old proud attitude. Her long arms hung motionless by her
> sides. Altogether she looked like some prisoner, falsely accused
> of a crime that she loathed and despised, and from which she
> was too indignant to justify herself.

Here is a heroine on the classic scale, defiant, icy,
melting by turns, who measures the world by her own
lofty standards, and understands no other yardstick. But if
Margaret Hale's strong feelings would cause embarrassment
at Cranford card parties, they are prized by Thornton, who
can reckon at first sight with the spirit he has to tame and
conquer. The ambitions of a self-made Northern manufacturer whose only assets are courage, industry and integrity
are stimulated by contact with the baffling, almost un-
approachable young woman from the South. Their union
is symbolic. Shadowed by his inflexible mother, Thornton
nourishes dreams of commercial power,

> Far away, in the East and in the West, where his person
> would never be known his name was to be regarded and his
> wishes to be fulfilled, and his word pass like gold.

So humiliation for him, too, is necessary :   reserve,

distance and haughty pride have to be demolished before
the two natures can be perfectly united. We know, indeed,
that in spite of their natural antipathies he and Margaret are
each other's fate ; that the attraction drawing them invisibly
together is as inevitable in its quality as the granite deter-
mination in his character and the inviolability of her soul.

Apart from this strong personal interest in *North and
South* the plot is well constructed, and served as the last
vehicle through which Mrs. Gaskell conveyed her distrust
at the presence in the world of so much misunderstanding.
Thus there are two conflicts which pursue their course along
parallel tracks. The personal struggle between Thornton
and Margaret, which ends in mutual capitulation, symbolises
the conflict between capital and labour, employer and
employee, industrial north and bourgeois south. Her
arguments for mediation between masters and men in
trade disputes are framed by Margaret's bewildered feelings
on first going to live among the strange society of Milton—
by which Manchester is implied. " I suppose," she says,
voicing Mrs. Gaskell's known views,

> " I suppose because, on the very face of it, I see two classes
> dependent on each other in every possible way, yet each
> evidently regarding the interests of the other as opposed to
> their own ; I never lived in a place before where there were
> two sets of people always running each other down."

But there are also other themes. The religious motive,
an intense preoccupation by the mid-century, is deliberately
given equal importance with the industrial problem. Mrs.
Gaskell, recalling perhaps her father's resignation on grounds
of principle from his ministry, poses the situation in reverse
before Mr. Hale. The recent case of Froude was also fresh
in her memory ; Mr. Hale resigns his living after much

heart-searching, and becomes a Dissenter. Margaret's interest in religious matters is strong. She is alive to the subtleties of conscience. She is morally precocious. It is precisely this quality in Mrs. Gaskell of apprehending such subtleties that caused Montégut's penetrating assessment :

> Mrs. Gaskell excelle comme on sait, à raconter ces affaires litigieuses de l'âme et tout ces petits procès intérieurs des facultés morales entre elles. C'est le romancier des cas de conscience.[1]

It is in *North and South* that one of the earliest of references is made to a projected factory canteen. Mrs. Gaskell's memory was good, and her observation acute. Faculties like these were a welcome addition to her imaginative powers. They have given us her fine set-pieces : Victorian interiors of all classes in town and village communities. A passage from *North and South* will preserve for future curiosity the principal living-room in a wealthy Manchester manufacturer's household of the 'fifties.

> There was no one in the drawing-room. It seemed as if no one had been in it since the day when the furniture was bagged up with as much care as if the house was to be overwhelmed with lava, and discovered a thousand years hence. The walls were pink and gold ; the pattern on the carpet represented bunches of flowers on a light ground ; but it was carefully covered up in the centre by a linen drugget, glazed and colourless. The window-curtains were lace ; each chair and sofa had its own particular veil of netting or knitting. Great alabaster groups occupied every flat surface, safe from dust under their glass shades. In the middle of the room, right under the bagged-up chandelier, was a large circular table, with smartly-bound books arranged at regular intervals around the circumference of its polished surface, little gaily coloured spokes of a wheel. Everything reflected light, nothing absorbed it.

[1] *Revue des Deux Mondes*, 1855.

IX

THE friendship existing between Mrs. Gaskell and Charlotte Brontë had flourished, perhaps not vigorously, yet with sincere literary admiration and personal interest. Their correspondence, warming, had led to a limited exchange of confidences and visits. In 1854 Miss Brontë became engaged to the Rev. A. B. Nicholls. In May, when she went to Leeds to buy her trousseau, she spent three days at Plymouth Grove. It was her last meeting with Mrs. Gaskell. She married ; nine months later she was dead.

She was hardly in her grave before the rumours began. Stories originating from her withdrawn existence began to disturb her friends. Ellen Nussey, anxious at this development, wrote off to Mr. Nicholls ; she felt decisive action to be necessary. He in turn consulted his father-in-law, and old Mr. Brontë, grudging yet convinced, invited Mrs. Gaskell to undertake an official *Life* and silence calumny.

The commission was accepted, work in hand was set aside. For two years she collected material, visited localities, examined correspondence, interviewed eye-witnesses. At the end of that time her book was complete. It appeared under the imprint of Smith, Elder, in February 1857, and in order to escape the critics, on the day of its publication, Mrs. Gaskell left England for the continent, accompanied by two of her daughters and Catherine Winkworth. It was the middle of February and they were bound for Rome.

They arrived as the Carnival was at its height. Their hosts, the William Wetmore Storys, received them at 43 via Sant' Isidoro, and this visit was the incidence of a friendship so nearly touching the emotions as to enrich Mrs. Gaskell's experience and fill her with recollections until the end of her life. There was an element of romance even in the manner of meeting.

The Storys had taken a balcony over the Corso to watch the Carnival. Below, in the packed street, seethed the Roman crowds. Colour and light were everywhere : the tumultous street sparkled with vitality.

Mrs. Gaskell, quickened by the excitement, permitted herself to dangle a long stick with confetti over the heads of the revellers. As she did so she became aware that someone was looking up at her, intently, out of the crowd. A young man caught at the confetti ; she exclaimed, " Oh, look, what a charming face " ; someone said, " That's Charles Norton."

A moment later he was among them, and being introduced. The scene is reconstructed in *A Dark Night's Work*, when Ellinor Wilkins first sees Canon Livingstone gazing up at her from the street below.

Charles Eliot Norton was thirty. Some years earlier the young New Englander had been presented to Mrs. Gaskell in London but had evidently made little impression. Now it was different. His circle was the Storys' : artists, sprinkled with a handful of literary dilettanti ; churchmen. Religious influences were, as ever, potent. Norton came of an intellectual Unitarian family, and was touring Europe. He was already a very enthusiastic admirer of Mrs. Gaskell's work. For her his friendship, rather earnest and spiritually intense, became linked with the happiest weeks of her life. Harmony seemed absolute, Manchester and reality were unreal and remote. Hardly a day passed without the interchange of

5

little notes : personal, subjective, verging on the sentimental, which the courier carried to and from the Piazza di Spagna and the via Sant' Isidoro. Daily meetings were fraught with anticipation ; the warmth of Norton's homage was as reviving as his bouquets.

The Storys gave breakfasts. Their guests were friends also of Norton's : cultured Americans, Englishmen living in Rome, Mgr. Manning, not yet a cardinal, Aubrey de Vere, the Fields of Philadelphia, Hamilton Wild.

The visit passed like a rapid and enchanted vision. All the suppressed emotionalism in Mrs. Gaskell's nature found its release that Roman spring. Gone was the Puritan, vanished the social reformer. Another element that lodged in her soul rose up and flowered, temporarily bathed in the light and poetry of Italy. It was precisely the impact of Roman traditions that confirmed her sense of hierarchy. At heart the Utilitarians among whom her lot was cast held little that she cared about. Her view of Christianity was by no means pronouncedly Nonconformist. "I, a sermon-hater," she was to write later to Norton. And she exclaims :

> "Now I like a smelling and a singing world. . . . I like Kings and Queens, and nightingales and mignonette and roses." [1]

She recognised herself for what she was : " mediaeval and *un*-Manchester, and un-American." We have few clues, but it is just possible that Catholicism interested her more than she would have cared to admit. With Norton, indeed, it was definitely discussed. Allusions, frequent throughout the novels and stories, are almost invariably sympathetic.

[1] Whitehill : *Letters of Mrs. Gaskell and Charles Eliot Norton.* 1932. p. 16.

Norton and Wild accompanied the party on their return journey as far as Venice, where they separated. Then the Gaskells themselves set out in a leisurely manner for home.

For her the Roman interlude was the most charming episode in her life : a culmination, in fact, of her experience. She had, she thought, never been so happy before. She felt she would never be so happy again.

The emotions are never static, and in its turn the tide of intensity ebbs. The friendship soon receded into proper perspective.

Norton returned that summer to America. Eventually he married. But the attachment so strenuously cultivated in those impressionable weeks was treasured by him, and fostered by correspondence kept up until Mrs. Gaskell's death.

For him there was something sacred in their friendship. More than fifty years later, when he, too, had died, it was found that he had preserved every scrap of writing associated with her ; letters, notes, pencilled messages, scribbled by her daughters in her name. Faithful to the end he was constant to his muse.

As the magic of the Italian weeks impressed her romantic memory so it was magnified by the subsequent contrast of her return to England and reality. From external light, colour and poetry supported by the pleasing devotion of a chivalrous young man, the enchanted traveller returned to the English climate, the critics, the threatened libel action. The effect of it all was, as Henry James said, " to embitter the after taste of the pleasure she had taken, in Rome, with so good a conscience."

The return journey was broken at various points. At the extreme end awaited a mountain of letters, many of which

were abusive. Like a chill wind the complications resulting
from the Brontë *Life* blew in cheerlessly upon her after the
languor and warmth of the south.

Once again she was overtaken by duties. It was the year
of the Manchester Exhibition, and with it came in succession,
responsibilities and distinguished visitors. She had to prepare
for the arrival of Harriet Beecher Stowe. At moments
desperation overcame her. What, for instance, was to be
done with Mr. Gaskell, who stuck so resolutely to his study,
and could not be induced to move ? There were times
when she wished he would go to America with Mr. Norton :
" I cd soon earn the passage and travelling money," she
writes. But of this there was to be no question. She, at
all events, felt constrained to face all comers at home with
a calm face and brave heart. Yet she dreaded the postman's
knock and the persistent rain of abusive letters.

The *Life of Charlotte Brontë* had, during her absence
abroad, met a barrage of criticism ; not because of its
literary merit which was unquestioned, but because, on a
number of counts, it had offended susceptibilities. Yet, after
emotions had subsided, after heart-burnings were healed and
offences repaired, it remained one of the strangest documents
in English biography. " It was," wrote Norton to Lowell,
" almost as much an exhibition of Mrs. Gaskell's character
as of Miss Brontë's."

It is remarkable purely as a story ; as a study of genius
it is inspired. Mrs. Gaskell's conclusions after that first
meeting at Low-wood had satisfied her ever-present instinct
for the dramatic. She created a living spirit out of an
otherwise remote figure at a time when curiosity was general.
It was soon satiated. Drama and pathos almost exceeding
description were revealed. No novel could exceed in

imaginative scope the burning yet morbid contrasts of the
Haworth setting. Mrs. Gaskell, indeed, made masterly use
of her sources. Though here and there over-dramatising in
order to heighten effects, and though writing subjectively,
for Norton's observation is certainly appropriate, it was
without doubt a work in which she fulfilled herself. There
was a side to her nature that relived the experiences of
others more violent than her own : thus the Brontë circle
satisfied her sense of the dramatic. Opportunities for
descriptive powers were unsurpassed : when she tells of
her bereft heroine alone in the stone-floored parlour on
winter nights, listening to the screaming wind about the
exposed Parsonage, when

> All the grim superstitions of the North, implanted in her by
> the servants during her childhood, returned with their burden
> of messages from the Dead . . .

there is no more sentimentality concerning death or the
dying. She rises to full height, and masters the essential
tragedy. Death here is paid its dues in full. Emily meets
it like a hero, Anne like a saint. Even Lady Eastlake's
damning review [1] of *Jane Eyre* receives deserved insignifi-
cance. Charlotte was insensitive to its wounds : " She
was numbed to all petty annoyances by the grand severity
of Death."

All, indeed, that Mrs. Gaskell had to tell of the sisters was
the result of intense imaginative sympathy. She understood
the delicate subtleties of character which gave them their
distinctness ; her definitions penetrated deeply :

" I distinguish reserve from shyness, because I imagine
shyness would please, if it knew how ; whereas reserve is

[1] *Quarterly*, 1848.

indifferent whether it pleases or not. Anne, like her eldest sister, was shy ; Emily was reserved."

A long distance has been travelled since the early prolixities.

Thus, an amazing subject was ready to hand. By the time her researches were complete and her evidence sifted she had material enough almost to write itself. Her personal selection should have been judiciously made, and the truth is that she was not always judicious. Indiscretion, as she had once admitted, was her besetting sin ; as such it now found her out on a number of counts. They were six in all.

She managed to offend Yorkshiremen by denigrating them in comparison with Lancastrians. She offended the Haworth servants by describing them as " rough, affectionate, warm-hearted, wasteful sisters." Here wasteful was the offending word. She libelled Mr. Brontë, representing him as a prey to ungovernable rages, and subject to accesses of carpet-burning and pistol-firing.

She was attacked by Mr. Carus-Wilson, the head of the Clergy Daughters' school, for damaging the reputation of his establishment.

She furnished a highly-coloured version of Branwell Brontë's moral decay, and of Mrs. Robinson's complicity.

She antagonised Mr. Nicholls, the husband of Charlotte Brontë. Indiscretion could go no further. The first edition of the *Life* was withdrawn, and the most libellous passages deleted. A full apology was printed in *The Times*, and the matter kept out of court.

Yet there is abundant evidence that her error was principally one of judgment. Certainly her statements were supported by Charlotte Brontë's two most intimate friends.

Mary Taylor, writing to Ellen Nussey with regard to subsequent editions of the *Life*, made the following comment :

> As to the mutilated section that is to come, I am sorry for it. Libellous or not, the first edition was all true, and, except the declamation, all, in my opinion, useful to be published.

Like most biographies published during the lifetime of many of the protagonists in a personal drama, the *Life* involved many delicate matters. But being infinitely superior to most other biographies, in itself, it blazed out of its notoriety into permanence. By its essential truth it atoned for lack of tact ; by its honesty its imprudence was redeemed. Psychologically it is a masterpiece, lit by the quality of understanding. The misanthropy, the courage, the constitutional pessimism of that extraordinary household are all intensified by Mrs. Gaskell's own warmth of feeling. There could be no pathos more tragic and intense than the picture she drew of the precocious children of Haworth parsonage silently dropping, one by one, into their moorside graves.

Charlotte is perpetuated : " A little, set, antiquated girl, very quiet in manners and very quaint in dress." The picture of precocity is unique ; the children with their intense imaginations seek every outlet for self-expression. Reading, writing, drawing, composing endless stories, assuming fantastic characters, taking their lonely exercise upon the moors, avoiding the village, flying from human contact. Strange, shy, uprooted Irish plants who " never faced their kind voluntarily, and always preferred the solitude and freedom of the moors."

In the field of English biography the *Life of Charlotte Brontë* is a classic. It has been ranked after Boswell's *Life of*

Johnson and Lockhart's *Life of Scott*. Nothing seems to justify a rearrangement. Its attraction is powerful ; much of it proceeds from its arrangement which is as orderly as Mrs. Gaskell's mind. Yet it was a mind with an ironical twist, and the intensely photographic vision of the innate gossip. And the gossip in her character recognised the authentic gossip in the souls of her old maids. In *Cranford*, this was an asset ; in the *Life*, a liability.

X

LITTLE was accomplished during the next few years. Worry, resulting from the *Life* appeared to have taken some of the heart out of Mrs. Gaskell's usual optimism. Between 1858 and 1864, the year of *Cousin Phillis* and *Sylvia's Lovers*, little but short stories and other miscellaneous contributions were published in the magazines. Latterly she had shown signs of resenting the editorial tyranny of Dickens, and had attempted to free herself from *Household Words*. She had begun writing for *Harper's* in 1858, and in 1860 for the *Cornhill*.

Of the bulk of her short stories there is little to be said. She wrote them assiduously, and when they were finished threw them into the ready maw of *Household Words* and its successors. They were easily thrown off, and as easily digestible. They fall chiefly into the pot-boiling category, and with one or two exceptions conform to certain types : those with a moral uplift, like the *Sexton's Hero* and *The Heart of John Middleton* ; those with an historical background like *Morton Hall*, and a miscellaneous collection of excellent thrillers and ghost-stories like *The Grey Woman* and *The Old Nurse's Story*. There is another very small category in which she displayed real originality : the best of these, *Curious if True*, was printed in the *Cornhill*.

There were also long short stories. Few in number, these contain some of her best character studies. Among them was *My Lady Ludlow*, which after appearing in *Household Words* in 1858 was embodied the next year in an assembly of tales, published by Sampson Low, as *Round the Sofa*.

My Lady Ludlow is in many ways akin to *Cranford*, but rambling, disconnected and less well planned. Superficially it lacks some of the obvious qualities which have given *Cranford* its great popularity. Yet in many respects it is more mature, more philosophical ; its humour is drier, its wit subtler. Its truths are profounder, its outlook altogether broader. *Cranford* immortalised the parochial scene ; *My Lady Ludlow* ennobles the village.

The central figure is Mrs. Gaskell's only complete portrait of the great lady of the old school, a type she refrained from developing in other books, and which therefore gains in delicacy by its isolation. It is a study of a wise old dowager, steeped in the aristocratic tradition, and believing in the exercises of responsibility and example as one of the essential functions of her order. It is in the dignity of that order that her pride is vested, never in herself. She therefore considers her own position objectively, as a trustee for her family and her caste.

Rich in her traditions her means are modest. The country house converted into a small academy for young ladies is a memory of Avonbank days with their plain living and high thinking.

Yet as a type Lady Ludlow is universal. She belongs to the great European tradition, and hers is a supremely civilised soul. A world, indeed, of custom divides her from the pretensions of the Honourable Mrs. Jamieson as it does from the obscurity of Lady Glenmire.

Mrs. Gaskell's other notable excursion into the peerage, Lady Cumnor of *Wives and Daughters*, is essentially a nineteenth-century product—harder, louder, more metallic. She is the advance guard of the Edwardian hostess, she is consequently less fine in her sentiments, her wisdom is wordly, tainted with material values.

In her that blend of breeding with insolence has developed which sometimes accompanies rank and expresses itself in a patronage demanding the best of both worlds. Dr. Gibson attends at The Towers for small fees because, as Lady Cumnor says,

> "It is such a thing for a man setting up in practice for himself to be able to say he attends at this house."

To the school and generation of Lady Ludlow such an attitude would have seemed the basest treachery of her order. But then she had been at the Court of Queen Charlotte. Inherent in her was the sense of being different. "People of rank," she used to say,

> "do not talk about their feelings, except to their equals, and even to them they conceal them, except upon rare occasions."

As a whole *My Lady Ludlow* contains jewels of Gaskell philosophy and humour. The prolonged French Revolution episode interferes sadly with the narrative and construction, diverts the attention and ruins the continuity ; otherwise the best *Cranford* methods are employed.

Most effective of all her devices for veiled irony is the employment of the objective narrator : the onlooker who relates the action as events unfold, but who at the same time professes ignorance of motive. Such are Mary Smith in *Cranford*, Paul Manning in *Cousin Phillis*, Margaret Dawson in *My Lady Ludlow*. These are the flies on the wall : naïve vehicles, quasi-innocents by means of whom we are introduced to the psychology of the unveiled heart.

Now Mrs. Gaskell's irony, if less acid, is by no means less astringent than Miss Austen's. Touching a raw spot it can smart, sometimes painfully. Dart after dart well aimed flies dead on to the target in *My Lady Ludlow*, a more pungent medium for social philosophy than *Cranford* (in which foolishness is to some extent the object of gentle ridicule). Mrs. Gaskell never presents her great ladies in a foolish light. Neither Lady Ludlow nor Lady Cumnor ever says a foolish thing. They have wisdom and brains. And if *Mary Barton* was the outlet for the reforming zeal in Mrs. Gaskell's nature, *My Lady Ludlow* is the confession of faith of her riper years and maturer judgment. In this study of the aristocratic tradition she yields to the arguments of hereditary sense. The wisdom is taken for granted.

Humour, irrepressible among her village scenes, works like yeast through the philosophy of *My Lady Ludlow*. Its chief virtue is in its accurate pointing ; its charm that it is delicately swathed in the Indian muslins of its time. It is all art. Take, for instance, the interview between Miss Galindo and Lady Ludlow who has offered her some secretarial duties connected with the estate, reluctantly accepted. " You know, perhaps," says Miss Galindo,

" that I was nearly being an authoress once, and that seems as if I was destined to employ my time in writing."

" No, indeed. . . . An authoress, Miss Galindo ! You surprise me."

" But, indeed, I was. All was quite ready. Doctor Burney used to teach me music ; not that I ever could learn, but it was a fancy of my dear father's. And his daughter wrote a book, and they said she was but a very young lady, and nothing but a music master's daughter ; so why should I not try ? "

" Well ? "

" Well. I got paper and half-a-hundred good pens, a bottle of ink, all ready."

" And then——"

" Oh, it ended in my having nothing to say, when I sat down to write. But sometimes, when I get hold of a book, I wonder why I let such a poor reason stop me. It does not others."

Miss Galindo is, on the whole, worth all the rest of Mrs. Gaskell's old maids put together. Though often cross, and always garrulous, she never fails to amuse, or to touch the heart by her loyalty and courage. For she is very human, more so even than Miss Matty. It is this which Lady Ludlow is so well able to appreciate ; she shows by discreet gestures how best to assist an old and impoverished friend. Yet Miss Galindo is not always easy to help ; as her benefactress knows, the responsibility which she feels toward her tenants and dependants is easier to exercise in the case of those whose social issues are clear cut. One of Lady Ludlow's secret advantages is that she is instinctively aware of the responsibility thrust upon her by her rank and influence. She knows when to change her opinion, to recant in the face of a mistake. When she interposes her authority with the magistrate on behalf of the poacher, we catch a gleam of the light that burnt so steadily in the recesses of Mrs. Gaskell's conscience. Once again it is the urge of justice, the recognition of generosity. This time she was more than fair. She was honouring a style of life as it dissolved before the reforming advance of her own generation. She herself snatched eagerly at its vanishing fabric. And Lady Ludlow, grown old in the grand manner, remained a perfect specimen under glass.

Miss Burney herself would not have been in any way a stranger to Mrs. Medlicott the housekeeper. She is one with that race of dragons whose knowledge of the intricacies of court etiquette made them such invaluable information centres. To the problem of precedence to be observed in the event of two Countesses' coaches meeting head-on in a narrow lane, Mrs. Medlicott, who had been bred in Germany, knew the answer : " De latest creation must back, for sure."

Nowhere else, perhaps, had Mrs. Gaskell a better occasion to explore a problem that lay close and constant at her heart : the claims of the classic and romantic approaches to society. She was torn between them, her heart beat for both. We can be by no means certain which side won the better of the argument. Lady Ludlow has some spirited trials of strength with the Rev. Mr. Gray, whose progressive ideas eventually win ; but the agent Mr. Horner's discomfiture is clearly argued. Lady Ludlow's prejudice against literacy in the working class is shown to proceed from a conception of feudal responsibility rather than from a sense of reaction. The boy whom Mr. Horner has trained to read and write against her wishes immediately abuses the privilege by reading a letter committed to his care. This lapse goes to strengthen her argument and confirm her apprehensions for the future of the nation. For where, indeed, is the advantage of education unless sustained by principle ? The agent's defence, that it is his eventual intention to train the boy to understand the rules of discretion calls out the full broadside of Lady Ludlow's logic :

"Trained ! Train a barn-door fowl to be a pheasant, Mr. Horner ! That would be easier talk. But you did right to speak of discretion rather than honour. Discretion looks to the consequences of actions—honour looks to the action itself, and is an instinct rather than a virtue. After all, it is possible you might have trained him to be discreet."

This is Mrs. Gaskell in all her strength and all her weakness. It is once again the story of her sense of fairness, and her belief in the ultimate triumph of moral values. She had in common with her generation a fundamental belief in the necessity for resignation, and to this belief she was loyal to the end of her life.

On the whole it is in this particular type of writing that her true self is revealed. And not only in *My Lady Ludlow*, but also in some of the other shorter works there came moments of inspiration. The impulse of pastoral emotion seems to effect a spiritual pregnancy, she becomes great with love for the scenes of her youth, mellowed, like the stones of Avonbank, by custom and memory. In this mood a fusion takes place of landscape and time-sense. This is particularly evoked by the Cheshire countryside. It is the Knutsford scene which of all others is so profoundly moving to her. And as transient memories are reclaimed from infancy she burnishes them with all the radiance of recollected feeling.

Not only by their innocent simplicity do her landscapes continue to charm, but by their essential truthfulness they perpetuate themselves, integrating common experience with cosmic vision until the whole receives an Arcadian grace. Thus the idyll is formed, as in *Cousin Phillis,* a flawless example of the sustained poetical mood. But there are other instances : some passages in *Wives and Daughters* have this especial quality, all directly inspired by the remembrance of childhood, and charged with tenderness for associations which will never return. But it is in a letter once written to Mary Howitt that the quintessence of this inner vision is contained. Nowhere else, perhaps, does serenity quite so enclose the secret microcosmic sense of childhood as in the following description of Old Tabley :

> Near the little, clean, kindly country town, where, as I said before, I was brought up, there was an old house with a moat within a park called Old Tabley, formerly the dwelling place of Sir Peter Leycester, the historian of Cheshire, and accounted a very fine specimen of the Elizabethan style. . . . Here on

summer mornings did we often come, a merry young party,
on donkey, pony, or even in a cart with sacks swung across—
each with our favourite book, some with sketch books, and
one or two baskets filled with eatables. Here we rambled,
lounged and meditated : some stretched on the grass in indolent
repose, half reading, half musing, with a posy of musk-roses
from the old-fashioned trim garden behind the house, lulled by
the ripple of the waters against the grassy lawn ; some in the
old crazy boats, that would do nothing but float on the glassy
water, singing, for one or two were of a most musical family,
and warbled like birds : " Through the greenwood, through
the greenwood," or " A boat, a boat, unto the ferry," or some
such old catch or glee. And when the meal was spread beneath
a beech tree of no ordinary size . . . one of us would mount
up a ladder to the belfry of the old chapel and toll the bell
to call the wanderers home. Then if it rained, what merry-
making in the old hall. It was galleried, with oak settles and
old armour hung up, and a painted window from ceiling to
floor. The strange sound our voices had in that unfrequented
stone hall !

Although this appears in one of her most fugitive pieces,[1] it
illustrates Mrs. Gaskell's extraordinary power of evoking in
the simplest language the romantic associations which have
been shared in some time or another by most imaginative
children. She drew upon the same source as early as *Mr.
Harrison's Confessions*, which contains an account of a
picnic, obviously at the same place, yet with how much less
of charm and emotion.

Knutsford, disguised in a variety of names, reappears
constantly as the model of the small country town, but
the disguise is usually slight. Identification is never
difficult even when it is not called Cranford. Knutsford
appears in *Mr. Harrison's Confessions* as Duncombe, in
Cousin Phillis as Eltham. It is the Hamley of *A Dark*

[1] Howitt, M., *Stray Notes from Mrs. Gaskell : Good Words*, 1895.

Night's Work, the Barford of *The Squire's Story*, the Hollingford of *Wives and Daughters*. The Drumble of *Cranford* is, of course, Manchester; so is the Milton of *North and South*. Monkshaven in *Sylvia's Lovers* is Whitby, and St. Sepulchre's transparently St. Cross, near Winchester.

XI

MRS. GASKELL, as middle age makes its gradual advance, seems to become rather more restless. Manchester sees less of her, and Mr. Gaskell goes his own way, refusing all persuasions to accompany his family on their foreign tours, preferring his solitary holiday as though relieved to be free of his bright encircling aviary. But pleasure was not the only reason for foreign travel. Her own health was deteriorating. In an attempt to escape the rigours of Manchester her visits to the continent were now prolonged in order to reduce the winter. She moved from place to place ; now in Germany, now in France ; almost invariably supported by a flotilla of daughters.

In 1858 they were at Heidelberg for three months. After that in Paris. There they were the guests of Mme. Mohl. Mme. Mohl, who had come into Mrs. Gaskell's life a few years earlier through the William Wetmore Storys was, although not yet the female Methuselah she eventually became, even then old enough to furnish a precious link with a palpitating epoch. For she had known Mme. Récamier, had diverted the decline of Châteaubriand and had once played a practical joke on Mme. de Staël. She had, too, been sought in marriage by Thiers, but had set her heart on Fauriel, while at the same time keeping the savant Julius Mohl for seventeen years in devoted suspense before finally bestowing herself and her wit upon him at the over-ripe age of fifty-four.

Afterwards, at the apartment in the Rue du Bac she

gave her famous Friday evenings. She was anti-Bonapartist, knew everybody and was surrounded by the fashionable and the learned. For the rest she herself was shabby and eccentric ; above all, amusing. Very, very amusing. Visits to Mme. Mohl became an increasing habit with Mrs. Gaskell.

Traces of Mohl influence are here and there to be found in various of the essays which appeared from time to time in *Household Words*, during the 'fifties. One of these is *Company Manners*, in which Mrs. Gaskell let off a few sparks from her observation of this conversational firework. It is an essay on that quintessence of cultural refinement, *Tenir un Salon*. The famous receptions of Mme. Mohl were among the last in a great French tradition, and to have known Mme. Mohl was to have forged a link with history. *Company Manners* is Mrs. Gaskell at her most discursive, and discursiveness, like the *espiègle* French bonnets she liked to wear, always suited her.

In 1859 she took her daughters to Whitby for part of the summer. Here she collected material for her projected new novel dealing with a local incident.

At the end of the eighteenth century, when the port's prosperity was based upon the whale fisheries—with a side-line in smuggling—and the lives of the townspeople were almost entirely linked with the fortunes of the whaling fleet, raids by the press-gang on the male population were active and therefore bitterly resented. *Sylvia's Lovers* has an *Enoch Arden* theme ; it is the drama of Sylvia Robson and her two suitors, Kinraid and Hepburn. Charley Kinraid, the sailor, is impressed but believed drowned ; Philip Hepburn, the landsman, marries Sylvia while withholding his knowledge that his preferred rival survives. Hepburn's subsequent struggle with his conscience provides the theme, developed systematically, which culminates in his expiation.

In the losing struggle his principles, theoretically high, are corrupted by his heart's desire. His conflict is one of conscience lulled by arguments in favour of his disastrous passion. Indeed, his craving for Sylvia dominating his existence is strong enough to smash his principles to the extent of wilfully deceiving her in respect of his former rival's intentions. Philip Hepburn, who works so deviously to obtain his lawful ends, is one of Mrs. Gaskell's most interesting creations. Psychologically his character is a work of art, always consistent because always true to type. In the end he inspires more respect than he deserves.

Sylvia's own problems are less involved. Her personal conflict is limited to her primitive love for Kinraid and loyalty to her parents. Not until the melodramatic end of the book does she behave with less consistency ; here her realisation of Hepburn's value and her appreciation of his virtues, although in keeping with the tragic atmosphere, can only be succeeded by death, for in a nature such as hers this change of heart would have been of temporary duration.

Mrs. Gaskell's true mission was not that of social reform, but of promoting understanding. The older she grew the wider her interest extended from the tribulations of oppressed groups to the infinitely subtle shades of the human soul. Loving-kindness, charity and a deep sympathy with the unlucky fellow in the condemned hold transfigure her work with the radiance of compassion. In the minutest reflections of mother and daughter after Daniel Robson has been committed for trial the agony of soul through which these women pass is unrelentingly shown. Robson hangs.

Overnight his wife becomes senile, his daughter turns from a flighty girl into a grave woman. Hepburn, their nearest relative, now their sole protector, thus benefits by his uncle's death, the women turn to him. By his marriage to Sylvia he obtains his ends, but as those ends are earthly, his marriage yields him nothing but dead sea fruit. So error is dragged by conscience through successive stages of the conflict. It is all, or almost all, to use the eighteenth-century phrase, *in nature*.

But towards the end of the story the whole fabric comes to pieces and falls apart. Events of the most unlikely character take place, and after Kinraid's sudden reappearance and Hepburn's flight the book concludes in a succession of wild and far-fetched improbabilities. The novelist appears suddenly to have tired of the story, and to have been seized with an overwhelming impulse to finish off the characters without quite knowing how to do it. The episodes dealing with the siege of Acre and the bedesmen of St. Sepulchre are the wild extravaganzas of a customarily sedate mind. Even so, she accomplished much. There is here an element missing from her earlier work ; it leads to speculation as to the direction in which, had she lived, this would have developed. It must certainly have continued. The wonder is how and why, at her mature age, did new horizons appear. There is one explanation to be offered. It is that, unconsciously, her study of the Brontës in their wild moorland setting influenced and gave her the power to create a work on a grander and fiercer scale than anything she had hitherto undertaken.

Sylvia's Lovers, impregnated with the flying spray and icy chill of the Greenland seas is remarkable for vivid colour and movement. The characters have, all of them, a more

vital intensity than those of the preceding novels, and this is
partly effected by a technical brilliance and verve unusual in
Mrs. Gaskell. It is without exception her most ambitious
work, differing from the rest, since it deals with a period
and locality involving detailed research. It is essentially
a romance of the sea and the soil. The Northumbrian
characters are primitive and sturdy, and considering that the
dialogue is almost entirely in accurate local dialect it is
surprisingly effective.

The story, wild and passionate in its elemental strength,
has something of symbolism in its nature. Love, Hate,
Revenge and Sacrifice thrive in their dramatic setting.
From a scholarly point of view the reconstruction of historical
events at Whitby is extremely well and carefully done. As
usual Mrs. Gaskell is mistress of her descriptive scenes. She
handles crowds with the skill of a film director, and with
much artistry. There is a surge of power in her description
of the activity down at the harbour when the whaling fleet
sails in :

> It was a pretty scene, though it was too familiar to the eyes
> of all who then saw it for them to notice its beauty. The sun
> was low enough in the west to turn the mist that filled the
> distant valley of the river into a golden haze. Above, on either
> bank of the Dee, there lay the moorland heights swelling one
> behind the other ; the nearer, russet brown with the tints of
> the fading bracken ; the more distant, grey and dim against
> the rich, autumnal sky. The red and fluted tiles of the gabled
> houses rose in crowded irregularity on the one side of the river,
> while the newer suburb was built in more orderly and less
> picturesque fashion on the opposite cliff. The river itself was
> swelling and chafing with the incoming tide till its vexed waters
> rushed over to the very feet of the watching crowd on the
> staithes, as the great sea waves encroached more and more every
> minute. The quay side was unsavourily ornamented with

glittering fish-scales, for the hauls of fish were cleansed in the open air, and no sanitary arrangements existed for sweeping away any of the relics of this operation.

The fresh salt breeze was bringing up the lashing, leaping tide from the blue sea beyond the bay. Behind the returning girls there rocked the white-sailed ship, as if she were all alive with eagerness for her anchors to be heaved. . . .

No one knew what might have happened. The crowd on shore grew silent and solemn before the dread of the possible news of death that might toll in upon their hearts with this up-rushing tide. The whalers went out into the Greenland seas full of strong, hopeful men ; but the whalers never returned as they sailed forth. . . . Whose bones had been left to blacken on the grey and terrible ice-bergs ? Who lay still until the sea should give up its dead ? Who were those who should come back to Monkshaven never, no, never more ?

Many a heart swelled with passionate unspoken fear, as the first whaler lay off the bar on her return voyage.

Molly and Sylvia had left the crowd in this hushed suspense. But fifty yards along the staithe they passed five or six girls with flushed faces and careless attire, who had mounted a pile of timber, placed there to season for ship-building, from which, as from the steps of a ladder or staircase, they could command the harbour. They were wild and free in their gestures, and held each other by the hand, and swayed from side to side, stamping their feet in time, as they sang—

> Weel may the Keel row, the Keel row, the Keel row,
> Weel may the Keel row that my laddie's in.

" What for are ye going off, now ? " they called out to our two girls. " She'll be in in ten minutes ! " and without waiting for the answer which never came, they resumed their song.

It might have been expected that *Sylvia's Lovers* would contain some allusion to local superstitions, but of superstitious practices and tales of the good-wife in general there is surprisingly little. Here, if ever, one might have expected this particular interest of Mrs. Gaskell's to blossom forth. But no such thing. The detail is based upon manners and customs of a certain district at a certain period, and accuracy in this respect has been recognised by competent judges.

There are a number of secondary characters in the story, all of them meticulously studied, and reproduced with the fidelity which was Mrs. Gaskell's strong point. Instead of the usual old family maid-servant, Kester, the cowman, fulfils his dour and devoted role. He gives advice, scorns reward, advances money from his savings when catastrophe overtakes the family, is faithful, practical and digressive. His utterances are full of hard-headed country wisdom.

The canvas is packed with other figures full of individual characterisation. The unconscious heroism of Hester Rose rings as true as does the slovenliness of the Corneys. John and Jeremiah Foster, the good Quaker mercers, are types of which the eighteenth century was never ashamed. With respectability on the counter and contraband in the back parlour they are inevitable yet incongruous, like a parson in the hunting field.

The remarkable use of dialect speech throughout the whole of *Sylvia's Lovers* stresses one aspect of Mrs. Gaskell's achievement in etymology, a taste she shared with her husband who was an authority on Lancastrian idiom.

All of her local folk-types, whether Manchester artisans or plain country people, talk in dialect, using local corruptions of an English which, once current, has now passed into disuse. The present work has neither scope nor space for a discussion of Mrs. Gaskell's employment of Northumbrian dialect, but the subject has been dealt with in some detail by Professor G. D. Sanders in his excellent study.[1] Her experimentations had certain positive results. She attempted successfully to present an aspect of English speech as used by

[1] *Elizabeth Gaskell*, Yale University Press, 1929.

certain distinct communities. She made a definite contribution to the existing knowledge of English dialect. She
led the way for later novelists in this particular field of
philology. To Dickens she owed nothing since she made
no encroachments in his cockney province. George Eliot
is really her first debtor ; but from George Eliot onward
the stream of provincial dialect in fiction widens until its
tributaries overflow into every part of the country. Daniel
Robson's whaling yarns are some of the most obviously
effective of Mrs. Gaskell's sustained passages of dialect. Here
he attempts to cap an adventure of Kinraid's, by one equally
imaginative :

"A were a specksioneer mysel, though, after that, a rayther
directed my talents int' t' smuggling branch o' my profession ;
but a were once a whaling aboord t' *Aimwell* of Whitby. An'
we was anchored off t' coast o' Greenland one season ; an'
we'd getten a cargo o' seven whale ; but our captain, he were
a keen eyed chap, an' niver above doin' any man's work ; an'
once seein' a whale he throws himself int' a boat an' goes off
to it, makin' signals to me, an' another specksioneer as were
off for diversion i' another boat, for to come after him sharp.
Well, afore we comes alongside, captain had harpooned t' fish ;
an' says he, 'Now, Robson, all ready ! give into her again
when she comes to t' top ' ; an' I stands up, right leg foremost,
harpoon all ready, as soon as iver I cotched a sight o' t' whale,
but niver a fin could a see. 'Twere no wonder, for she were
right below t' boat in which a were ; and when she wanted
to rise, what does t' great ugly brute do but come wi' her head,
as is like cast iron, up bang again t' bottom o' t' boat. I were
thrown up in t' air like a shuttlecock, me an' my line an' my
harpoon—up we goes, an' many a good piece o' timber wi'
us, an' many a good fellow too ; but a had t' look after mysel',
an' a were up high i' t' air, afore I could say Jack Robison, an'
a thowt a were safe for another dive int' saut water ; but
i'stead a comes down plump on t' back o' t' whale. Ay' yo'
may stare, master, but theere a were, an' main an' slippery it

were, only a sticks my harpoon intil her an' steadies mysel',
an' looks abroad o'er t' vast o' waves, an' gets sea-sick in a
manner, an' puts up a prayer as she mayn't dive, and it were
as good a prayer for wishin' it might come true as iver t'
clargyman an' t' clerk too puts up i' Monkshaven church . . .
but at last t' harpoon broke, an' just i' time, for a reckon she
was near as tired o' me as a were on her, and down she went ;
an' a had hard work to make for t' boats as was near enough
to catch me ; for what wi' t' whale's being but slippery an' t'
watter being cold, an' me hampered wi' t' line an' t' piece o'
harpoon, its a chance, missus, as thou had stopped an oud
maid.'

There is much more ; it is, like the rest of the monologues
in dialect, extremely well done, ingenious, but in the long
run a little monotonous.

For all her talent Mrs. Gaskell is not a very quotable
writer. This is to say that quotation away from its context
is apt to suffer. The effect of her writing is above all
cumulative ; passages illuminating to the reader convey
relatively little to those who are unfamiliar with her work.
Verbosity, for instance, a familiar trait, repeatedly takes the
heart out of her dialogue. Conciseness is, with her, not a
natural virtue. In description she relied upon detail dear to
her heart ; a painter anticipating a photographic accuracy.
The leaf is veined, and shaded in as delicately as in one of
Mrs. Loudon's flower pictures. The drawing, if accurate, is
apt to be over-elaborate.

Her prose at all times lacks terseness and elegance. Her
style is occasionally clumsy and her chronology careless. Her
approach is not that of the pure artist. Yet the full flavour
of her spirit pervades the whole of her important work,
though extracts fail to convey this essential quality, and it is
characteristic that her most satisfying effects are gained from
a common experience easily recognised. So for her most

telling passages quotation, brief quotation at least, is baffling
and elusive. Of the dialogue this is especially true. Her wit
is dependent in a subtle degree upon the interplay of question
and answer. Not in the sharp incisiveness of repartee. It
turns more on a knowledge of the characters than on any
individual specimen. It is in *Cousin Phillis*, for instance,
that an exquisite example occurs in which, as so often
happens, fancy is snubbed by reality. This is when Holdsworth, enamoured and conciliatory, wishes to paint Phillis
with a wreath of wheat-ears in her hair.

> " You would like," he asks her mother, " You would like a
> portrait of your daughter as Ceres, would you not, Ma'am ? "
> " I should like a picture of her ; yes, very much, thank you,
> Mr. Holdsworth ; but if you put that straw in her hair you'll
> ruffle her hair. Phillis, my dear, if you're to have your picture
> taken, go upstairs and brush your hair smooth."

Imperturbable Victorians, to whom pretentiousness was
so alien and simplicity so natural. This is not great art but
it is fine understanding of the little subtle processes by means
of which interior situations are sown, born and developed.

The spring of 1862 had been spent touring Normandy
and Brittany with Meta and a friend. There was also the
usual visit to Paris, inevitably to Mme. Mohl. Some
account of these travels [1] was published two years later. By
early summer the party were back in London for the
Exhibition, thereafter going home. But in America Civil
War had begun. In Manchester its repercussions were felt
in the mills, and demonstrated by famine. Autumn and
winter that year were nightmare seasons. Enlisting her
daughters for support Mrs. Gaskell began organising relief
for the destitute. The work was exacting and exhausting.

[1] *French Life, Fraser's Magazine*, 1864.

It continued day after day. The family were out each morning and at their duties till nightfall. Then, worn out, too tired to eat, they returned only to drop into their beds. The result of all this might not have been unexpected. Mrs. Gaskell overtaxed her health and broke down. It was the first serious crack in the energetic system. She was obliged to rest ; she went south, to the seaside, and restored herself at Eastbourne.

XII

DURING the interval between 1859 and 1863, years spent in the leisurely preparation of *Sylvia's Lovers*, a fair number of short stories made their initial appearance either in *All the Year Round* or the *Cornhill*. Of these the most characteristic are *Six Weeks at Heppenheim*, *A Dark Night's Work* and *Cousin Phillis*. They appeared in 1862-3, all are in varying degrees rewarding ; the first and the last especially, both love stories, have an indefinable grace and tenderness besides being in a high degree remarkable for the atmosphere they convey. In *Six Weeks at Heppenheim* a Rhineland village shimmers in the vintage season, and is as relaxed in mood as a prolonged convalescence.

A Dark Night's Work, a fairly long short story, appeared in the early months of 1863 in *All the Year Round*. It is still enjoyable, partly on account of its suspense, but also for the well-conceived character of Mr. Wilkins, for Ellinor who belongs to the same race as Margaret Hale, and for the Carnival scenes in Rome. Dixon, the gardener, is one of the gallery of superb domestic types. Mr. Wilkins is sufficiently un-Gaskellian to be interesting on that score alone ; though his family and its avocations are repeated in those of Mr. Dudgeon in *The Squire's Story* one cannot call to memory another example of the parvenu whose dilettante temperament pushed to extremes leads him to commit manslaughter. There is, however, a flat note of anti-climax in the introduction of the clerical hero, Canon Livingstone.

The outstanding work of this period was the sublime little idyll in which harmony is the chief quality. *Cousin Phillis*, in art, observation and economy of phrasing, in human knowledge and in serenity, equals *Cranford*. It is not otherwise comparable since the one is a story, the other a series of papers. *Cousin Phillis*, with its absence of direct action, its reflectiveness and emotional tension, is itself not so much a story as a tragic episode in the life of a girl. It consists of a tale of first love, its secrecy, its deception and its consequences ; no more. Only an unfaltering technique such as Mrs. Gaskell had come in her later books to perfect could have succeeded in giving its particular vague fragrance to this country bouquet. There are no false steps either in taste or execution. Feeling, always her surest guide, pervades the whole. And here she is back again in her pastoral mood. The scene is the Knutsford district : Hope Farm is Sandlebridge. In Phillis's father, Ebenezer Holman—who successfully combines the practice of his faith with his occupation—an echo is distantly heard of William Stevenson, also sometime minister and farmer. When Farmer Holman is first discovered by Paul Manning in his fields at sunset gathering his labourers around him there is a note in the eternal simplicity of the scene which could only have sprung from an Evangelical source.

> Suddenly changing the tone of his deep bass voice to an odd suggestion of chapels and preachers, he added, " Now I will give out the psalm, ' Come all harmonious tongues,' to be sung to ' Mount Ephraim ' tune ! "
> He lifted his spade in his hand, and began to beat time with it ; the two labourers seemed to know both words and music, though I did not ; and so did Phillis : her rich voice followed her father's as he set the tune ; and the men came in with more uncertainty, but still harmoniously. Phillis looked at me once

or twice with a little surprise at my silence ; but I did not know the words. There we five stood, bareheaded, excepting Phillis, in the tawny stubble-field, from which all the shocks of corn had not yet been carried—a dark wood on one side where the wood-pigeons were cooing ; blue distance seen through the ash-trees on the other. Somehow, I think that if I had known the words, and could have sung, my throat would have been choked up by the feeling of the unaccustomed scene.

Emotion is never distant from Mrs. Gaskell's work. There are times when it is redundant, others when it is misplaced. But in such a passage as this, when it is bridled by an exactness approaching understatement, she achieves a perfection of balance which has made *Cousin Phillis* into the little gem it is. Pathos, an effect so hard to achieve, so easy to defile, is implicit in the haunting narration of Phillis's lost illusions. For she is no usual farmer's daughter. Quiet, contemplative and reserved, she is drawn to books for her interest and her recreation. "I took down," says Paul Manning, "one or two of those books once when I was left alone in the house-place on the first evening—*Virgil*, *Caesar*, a Greek grammar—oh, dear ! ah, me ! and Phillis Holman's name in each of them."

Paul Manning, like Mary Smith in *Cranford*, is the medium ; through him Phillis's nature is made known. All the little subtleties which lend her delicacy are interpreted by his bluntly youthful observations. Yet Paul has himself a fineness of feeling which no amount of blundering can destroy. In introducing Edward Holdsworth to the family at Hope Farm he wishes, boyishly, to impress both his cousins and his hero. The consequences are naturally disastrous, and Phillis is the victim. There is a moral to all this. Minister Holman and his wife, by their refusal to admit the fact that Phillis is no longer a child but a free and independent individual, are thus robbed of her confidence and stricken by her despair. However they may reproach Paul Manning the fault is theirs ; theirs the responsibility for their own over-possessiveness. It is Paul himself, not the parents, who understands the tragedy of Phillis's young feelings. Herein lies a purity of touch which gives the little work an elect quality that is all of its own. It resembles nothing else, for it is unique.

Mrs. Gaskell's connection with the *Cornhill* had begun in 1860. Since then the policy of the editor, George Smith, had been the doubling of fees in order to secure his contributors' best efforts. In 1864 he commissioned from her a novel for which he offered £2000 for a seven-year copyright. One more, her last and ablest work of fiction, went into preparation. She called it *Wives and Daughters*.

In the choice of almost all her titles she displayed the same lack of imagination that determined those names which somehow handicap her most effective characters. A dowdiness is apparent like that belonging to a wardrobe of good but never quite fashionable clothes. Here again, comparison with George Eliot springs to mind ; the bold imagination of *Middlemarch*, the curious stimulus of *Daniel Deronda*, as titles, are powerful foils to the colourless sound of their opposite numbers. For it is through George Eliot, the name most associated in literary comparison with Mrs. Gaskell, that a final assessment is most conveniently obtained. Both women sprang from the strong dissenting circles of the Midlands, both were interested in social problems, both wrote of provincial life. That they differed upon certain fundamental issues that arose in the course of nineteenth-century ethical philosophy goes only to strengthen their complementary value to one another. Taken together they form a valuable contrast—although there appears to be some doubt whether they ever met in person—the one supplying what the other lacked. The one is powerful, the other gentle ; the one intellectual, the other emotional. Both are exponents of characterisation, both conscious of the intransigeance of Progress. Here the advanced theories supported by George Eliot held no attraction for Mrs. Gaskell : she was immovable, for instance on sex equality, and only with reluctance signed the petition for the Married Women's Property Act. But she acknowledged and recognised her artistic superior :

> I have a feeling (she wrote to Norton) that it is not worth while trying to write, while there are such books as *Adam Bede* and *Scenes from Clerical Life*.[1]

However uninspired her choice, the title *Wives and Daughters* is characteristic of Mrs. Gaskell. There is no particular reason for it, and although wives and daughters are certainly concerned in the plot it equally concerns husbands and sons, fathers and mothers, brothers and half-sisters. It is in any case quite unsuggestive of the radiant and superbly executed novel of English manners which inaugurated what would undoubtedly have been a new phase in Mrs. Gaskell's literary career. It is the first to be completely free from religious interest, conveys no message, concerns no problems, but is a straightforward love story, cunningly devised and intricately woven. The construction is splendid, and her interplay of action and development worked out with a precision that places it technically in the front rank with the masterpieces of domestic fiction. It is lengthy. Latterly there are signs of weariness ; the writer herself confessed to being tired of the story as it spun itself

[1] Whitehill : *Letters of Mrs. Gaskell and Charles Eliot Norton*. 1932. p. 39.

out toward its abrupt, unfinished close. But she was nearing the end of her life ; she was not unaware that, like Osborne Hamley, she, too, might be overtaken, swiftly, suddenly and without a sign.

Wives and Daughters is an eightsome. There are four pairs of characters, four of them men, four of them women. Four are elderly ; four are youthful. They appear against the background of county and provincial life in the early years of the last century, and their fortunes are all more or less involved with those of Molly Gibson, the unsophisticated heroine whose solid integrity and charming candour are a development of Maggie Browne of *The Moorland Cottage*.

The value of *Wives and Daughters* is greater at present than on its original appearance since dealing with no contemporary problems it depends for its effect upon the innumerable little circumstantial details which give it its essentially English character. Life is shown in a day-to-day description as it was lived in a small country town during the last century. For her setting Mrs. Gaskell turned once again to the unfailing source of her childhood's happiness : Knutsford. This time it appears as Hollingford, and she represented faithfully the proceedings of English country life in three layers of society : the aristocracy, the landed gentry and the professional middle classes. That their fortunes are inextricably involved is owed entirely to the personality of the heroine. For, if Molly Gibson had lacked the personal qualities linking her on the one hand to the Cumnors and on the other to the Hamleys, there would have been little story to develop. The plot results from the most intuitive observation of character, there are two sets of personalities. Individuals in the foreground are superimposed upon a back cloth teeming with types mostly drawn from the stock of preceding tales of Knutsford life.

The story, crammed with contemporary domestic detail, radiates from the characters of the two half-sisters, their family and their love affairs, and introduces, in the character of the ex-governess Clare, one of the most brilliantly effective and subtle portraits in English fiction. What makes her so particularly convincing is her astounding truth to nature. It is this truth that makes the creation of Clare something of a work of art. She is not, like her predecessor, Becky Sharp, a caricature. Instead, and even allowing for a similarity of character, there is an engaging aspect to this absurdly pretentious creature that is totally wanting in Becky. Clare is almost as unscrupulous and nearly as cold in her calculations. She is selfish, but not cruel. After all, though she schemes to marry Mr. Gibson—just as she no doubt schemed to marry poor Mr. Kirkpatrick—there is something really most disarming about the helpless little woman who describes herself as having always been a " kind of pet with gentlemen." Even Molly cannot long be jealous of the intruder, though Clare's affectations are exasperating to her solid commonsense :

"I remember a little poem of Mr. Kirkpatrick's, in which he compared my heart to a harpstring, vibrating to the slightest breeze."

"I thought harpstrings required a pretty strong finger to make them sound," said Molly.

"My dear child, you've no more poetry in you than your father."

Really, one's heart warms to the ridiculous illogical creature. She had lived for so long by her wits, and had so well proved her worth as an appendage of the

Cumnors, that she felt entitled to her share of comfort and independence, and most of all to social respect. She had been something of a beauty, and she felt robbed of her birthright :

> Her beautiful hair was of that rich auburn that hardly ever turns grey ; and partly out of consciousness of its beauty, and partly because the washing of caps is expensive, she did not wear anything on her head ; her complexion had the vivid tints that often accompany the kind of hair which has once been red ; and the only injury her skin had received from advancing years was that the colour was rather more brilliant than delicate, and varied less with every passing emotion.

She had been, too, a great favourite as governess at The Towers :

> So ready to talk, when a little trickle of conversation was required ; so willing to listen . . . with tolerable intelligence, if the subjects spoken about did not refer to serious solid literature, or science, or politics, or social economy. About novels and poetry, travels and gossip, personal details, or anecdotes of any kind, she always made exactly the remarks which are expected from an agreeable listener ; and she had sense enough to confine herself to those short expressions of wonder, admiration and astonishment, which may mean anything, when more recondite things were talked about.

Mr. Gibson is the very man to be caught by this sort of assumed ingenuity. His belief in reason as the lord of all leads him up one or two garden paths, and matrimony with Clare turns out to be a blind alley. He is the final justification for the many studies done by Mrs. Gaskell of the old-fashioned country practitioner. If in her youth she originally gained her experience by observing her uncle Dr. Peter Holland, she certainly did not confine herself to a single portrait. No two characters among her country doctors are alike ; all are individual. One quality they share however, to the absolute degree. They are all conscientious and honest. Of the other men in *Wives and Daughters*, Squire Hamley, though closely detailed is less clear-cut ; Lord Cumnor with his vague mannerisms is the more convincing personality.

> Lord Cumnor seldom passed anyone of his acquaintance without asking a question of some sort—not always attending to the answer ; it was his mode of conversation. . . .

There is at times a note not entirely devoid of malice. The Cumnors provide much ammunition for ridicule, and it is in part justified. Capital is made out of the humbler people who enjoy being impressed. The disappointment caused among the beholders when the duchess arrives at the ball is acute. They had waited up half the night to see a duchess in family diamonds ; they were rewarded with the entry of a stout, elderly woman in sprigged muslin, and without a single gem.

Such is vanity, and such are illusions. Mrs. Gaskell understood her fellow-beings and was sometimes a little impatient. Her own experiences are constantly brought to bear upon the situations she created. Conscious of her father's evident mistake she alludes bitterly to remarriage, and Molly's sense of outraged possessiveness is an emotion that can have been no stranger to her. The same point is stressed in an earlier tale, *The Doom of the Griffiths*. There is a personal note about Molly Gibson which supports the idea that she may be partly a self-portrait. Certainly her affinity with Maggie Browne exists, and Maggie Browne inspired Maggie Tulliver in more than one respect. Yet the ravishing Cynthia is infinitely more interesting because, like

her mother, she is more subtle ; her appeal is rather through
her failings than through her qualities.

> "It's no use talking," she says to Molly, "I am not good,
> and I never shall be now. Perhaps I might be a heroine still,
> but I shall never be a good woman, I know . . ."

and again,

> "But don't you see I have grown up outside the pale of
> duty and 'oughts.' Love me as I am, sweet one, for I shall
> never be better."

The action of *Wives and Daughters* is intended to take place
some forty-five years before the time of writing. But the
confusion arriving from Mrs. Gaskell's chronology suggests
a few observations. She had in fact, a careless attitude
towards years, names and ages. Frequently they are impossible to reconcile. With the exception of *Sylvia's Lovers*
in which, regarding details, she had taken great care, her
slapdash methods were the result of trusting an unreliable
memory. Presumably, once the serial parts of her novels
had been despatched, she kept no reference and forgot much
(to her) unimportant detail. *Cranford* is this respect does not
bear examination. It bristles with chronological inexacti-
tudes. And *Wives and Daughters* is a maze of minor con-
fusions. If, on the basis of her statement, the events at the
beginning of the story take place forty-five years earlier,
when Molly Gibson is twelve, then that year must be 1820.
But a little later Molly is seventeen and wearing a flimsy
plaid silk of no known clan tartan. This would appear to
be an unlikely type of dress, since the indiscriminate wearing
of tartans by the laity suggests the era of Balmoral rather
than that of the Brighton Pavilion. At any rate the year
would still be only 1825, and mention is here made of a

concert given by Grisi. But Grisi, born in 1812, never set foot in England before 1834. Again, the entire action of the book occupies about three years so that it would still be only about 1828 by the close of the story. Yet Osborne Hamley's baby is born and christened sometime in the 1830's, and his brother Roger returns from Africa with a fine sweeping Darwinian beard. In fact the whole flavour of the book is thoroughly mid-Victorian, and as such was anachronistically illustrated by du Maurier. There are other peculiarities familiar to students of Mrs. Gaskell's stories : her characters have sometimes a disturbing habit of forgetting their own names. Miss Browning starts off as Clarinda but ends as Dorothy ; in *Cousin Phillis* a similar mishap occurs to the two maiden ladies who make their debut as the Misses Brown but are later metamorphosed into the Misses Dawson.

Most glaring of all : Mr. Kirkpatrick is, in the year 1827, described as a Q.C. But what of that ? At the time of writing Mrs. Gaskell's daughter had recently married Charles Crompton, a young Q.C., and the parallel was probably in her mind.

In 1864 she had spent part of the summer at Pontresina. There, in a quiet room outside the village, *Wives and Daughters* was begun. In the autumn she fell ill. For three months she was almost perpetually indoors, despairing at times of recovery until, in the following year and after one more visit to Mme. Mohl, she was able to write to Norton :

> I did a terribly grand thing ! and a secret thing too. Only you are in America and can't tell. I bought a house and 4 acres of land in Hampshire—near Alton—for Mr. Gaskell to retire to and for a home for my unmarried daughters.[1]

[1] Whitehill : *Letters of Mrs. Gaskell and Charles Eliot Norton.* 1932. p. 125.

This house, The Lawn, at Holybourne, was bought with the earnings of *Wives and Daughters*. Its cost was £2600, part of which was advanced on mortgage by her publishers, Smith and Elder. For three years it was to be let, after which William Gaskell, then over sixty, was to take possession with the two unmarried daughters ; Marianne was by this time engaged to her cousin, Thurstan Holland.

The transaction was to be kept secret until the redemption of the mortgage, when the property was to be formally presented to its future owner. In her own mind and implicit in her words was Mrs. Gaskell's presentiment, strengthened by recent illness, that she herself might not be spared to share the life at The Lawn. The breadwinner's protective instinct betrayed itself.

By the autumn *Wives and Daughters* was all but finished. She had reached Chapter LX, in which Roger Hamley discovers his true feelings, and provokingly sets off again for darkest Africa, while Molly, dodging behind her stepmother's gesticulations, waves him farewell from the window. There is not much more to be said, and Mrs. Gibson chatters away with benevolent affability until she is tired out with scheming and planning, and wishes only for a rest. She is still speaking when the story breaks off . . .

" and now cover me up close, and let me go to sleep, and dream about my dear Cynthia and my new shawl. . . ."

No more was ever written by Mrs. Gaskell. Quite suddenly the end came. She was down at Holybourne visiting the new house with her son-in-law and two of her daughters. It was Sunday, November 12, 1865. There had been church in the morning ; in the afternoon some discussion of plans. Later, tea was brought into the drawing-room where they were all sitting. One of the daughters handed a cup of tea to her mother on the sofa—she had been speaking until that moment. But there was no response. Only the head falling forward abruptly in that instant gave warning that all was over. It was just as she had, in one of those luminous moments, written years before of Mrs. Hilton in *Ruth* :

> They found her lying dead on her accustomed sofa. Quite calm and peaceful she lay ; there had been no struggle at last : the struggle was for the survivors.

She was buried at Knutsford a few days later in the ground of the Unitarian Chapel. By far the finest monument to her memory is the collection of first editions of her published works, now in the Knutsford library.

Wives and Daughters was concluded, briefly and lucidly, by Frederick Greenwood, then editor of the *Cornhill*. It was a synthesis of Mrs. Gaskell's known intentions as to the outcome of the story, gained from her daughters' knowledge.

In her campaigns for tolerance, which are never militant but always advocatory, she firmly opposed all hatred, bigotry and narrow nationalism, whether political or religious. Again and again she exposed ignorance, the uncharitableness of the insular and parochial temper. Squire Hamley of *Wives and Daughters* is a case in point, with his hatred of Frenchmen and Catholics. The Vicar of Monkshaven, too, in all other respects a mild man, is an example of Nationalism in the Established Church. He is affected by his hatred and fear of the French and the Dissenters. These are types which, in a later age, Mrs. Gaskell would have pounced upon, and as effectively ridiculed. For having herself no hatred in her heart she found anything other

than the Christian solution unthinkable. The Vicar of
Monkshaven could usefully illustrate her views ; he

> had two bugbears to fear—the French and the Dissenters. It
> was difficult to say of which he had the worst opinion and the
> most intense dread. Perhaps he hated the Dissenters most,
> because they came more in contact with him than the French ;
> besides, the French had the excuse of being Papists, while the
> Dissenters might have belonged to the Church of England if
> they had not been utterly depraved.

Could she, could she for a moment have had in mind the
Rev. Mr. Nicholls, whose hatred of Dissenters was so strong
and so prejudiced that Charlotte Brontë had not dared go
to chapel with the Gaskells ?

Then again, Squire Hamley, a John Bull with a pedigree,
surpasses the Vicar of Monkshaven in the violence of his
views. The French are, to him, anathema. Even an essay
in a learned French journal, concerning his son's scientific
discoveries, rouses all his latent intense nationalism. " I'd
ha' let him alone ! " he says, earnestly. " We had to beat
'em, and we did it at Waterloo ; but I'd not demean myself
by answering any of their lies, if I was you." In principle
he detested all foreigners, " and moreover held all Roman
Catholics in a dread and abomination something akin to our
ancestors' dread of witchcraft."

As she knew, it is the lot of the primitive type to suffer
uncontrollably in moments of humiliation. The price old
Hamley pays is high indeed. Complacent in his family
pride, and aggressive in his faith, he has to endure the greatest
mortification of all. In the death of the heir whom he has
estranged but still idolises, humiliation is absolute. He
discovers Osborne to have been married in secret, and to
have left behind him a wife who in every respect is an

outrage to his dearest prejudices. She is French, she is of an inferior class, worse still, she is a papist. But Mrs. Gaskell seldom appeals ineffectually to compassion. In spite of his undisciplined nature Squire Hamley is a likeable, explosive, peppery and sentimental old tyrant, and he learns his lesson and makes amends in generous style.

Throughout Mrs. Gaskell's work the idea of understanding is strong and pervasive. It is precisely this idea which fired her early phase of social indignation and mellowed her later period of detached and observant humour. There is nothing spectacular about her work or personality. In an age of literary brilliance this unassuming yet steadfast luminary tended to be dimmed by the proximity of the great surrounding planets, her contemporaries. Yet at her best her writing reflects virtues not easily found among those with even the greatest reputations. They embody her own remedy for the attainment of human happiness. Her prescription, by no means new, was to her mind simple and obvious, compounded from three basic elements. It contained Faith, Hope and Charity. To her as well, the greatest of these was Charity.

BIBLIOGRAPHY

Elizabeth Gaskell. By GERALD DE WITT SANDERS, Ph.D. With a bibliography by Clark S. Northup, Ph.D. [Yale University Press : (O.U.P.)]. 1929.

Mrs. Gaskell : Haunts, Homes and Stories. By E. A. CHADWICK. 1910.

Mrs. Gaskell and her Friends. By E. HALDANE. 1930.

Memorials of Two Sisters. By M. T. SHAEN. 1908.

Letters of Mrs. Gaskell and Charles Eliot Norton, 1855–1865. Ed. by JANE WHITEHILL. 1932.

Mary Howitt : An Autobiography. 2 vols. 1889.

CHRONOLOGY

1810.   Born in Chelsea, Sept. 29.

1811.   Removed to her aunt's at Knutsford.

1825–7. At school at Avonbank, Stratford-upon-Avon.

1832.   Marries Rev. William Gaskell at Knutsford.

1837.   *Sketches Among The Poor.* *Blackwood's.* January.

1840.   Attracts notice of Wm. Howitt, who prints her account of Clopton House in his *Visits to Remarkable Places.*

1848.   *Mary Barton* published and acclaimed by world of letters.

1850.   Invited by Dickens to contribute to *Household Words.*
        Meets Charlotte Brontë at Briery Close.
        The Moorland Cottage published.

1851.   Charlotte Brontë visits the Gaskells in Manchester.

1853.   *Cranford* and *Ruth* published.
        Visits Charlotte Brontë at Haworth.
        Visits Mme. Mohl in Paris.

1855.   *North and South.* Prepares *Life of Charlotte Brontë.*

1857.   *Life of Charlotte Brontë* published.
        Visits Rome. Meets C. E. Norton.

1858.   *My Lady Ludlow* appears in *Household Words.*

1862.   Overstrains herself organising relief for Manchester destitute.

1864.   *Cousin Phillis* and *Sylvia's Lovers* published.

1865.   Buys The Lawn, Holybourne, near Alton.
        While staying there dies suddenly, Nov. 12.
        Buried in yard of Unitarian Chapel, Knutsford, Nov. 16.

1866.   *Wives and Daughters* published posthumously.

WORKS BY MRS. GASKELL

Life in Manchester (1848).
Mary Barton, a Tale of Manchester Life, 2 vols. (1848).
The Moorland Cottage (1850).
Ruth, 3 vols. (1853).
Cranford (1853).
Lizzie Leigh and other Tales (1854).
North and South, 2 vols. (1855).
The Life of Charlotte Brontë (1857).
My Lady Ludlow (1858).
Round the Sofa, 2 vols. (1859).
Right at Last, and other Tales (1860).
A Dark Night's Work (1863).
Sylvia's Lovers, 3 vols. (1863).
Cousin Phillis and other Tales (1865).
The Grey Woman and other Tales (1865).
Wives and Daughters, 2 vols. (1866).

INDEX